The Great Florida Seminole Trail

Complete Guide to Seminole Indian Historic and

Cultural Sites Open to the Public

Pineapple Press, Inc.
Sarasota, Florida

Inquiries should be addressed to:

Pineapple Press, Inc.
P.O. Box 3889
Sarasota, Florida 34230

www.pineapplepress.com

ISBN 978-1-56164-563-3 (paperback)
ISBN 978-1-56164-616-6 (e-book)

Library of Congress Cataloging-in-Publication Data

Alderson, Doug.
  The great Florida Seminole trail : complete guide to Seminole indian historic and cultural sites open to the public / by Doug Alderson.
     p. cm.
  Includes bibliographical references and index.
  ISBN 978-1-56164-563-3 (pbk. : alk. paper)
  1. Seminole Indians--History--Guidebooks. 2. Seminole Indians--Antiquities--Guidebooks. 3. Indian trails--Florida--Guidebooks. 4. Florida--Guidebooks. I. Title.
  E99.S28A774 2013
  975.9004'973859--dc23
                        2012031264

First Edition
10 9 8 7 6 5 4 3 2 1

Design by Shé Hicks
Printed in the United States of America

All photos not otherwise credited were taken by the author.

All maps were created by the author.

Front cover photo of a diorama at the Ah-Tah-Thi-Ki Museum on the Big Cypress Seminole Reservation (Doug Alderson). Author photo on back cover by Jan Corcoran.

Contents

Harvard Burney has been a Seminole reenactor for more than a decade.

Preface

A t some point, as you follow this guide to historic and cultural sites related to the Seminole Indians, the Seminole experience in Florida may hit home. Seminole Indians are a tiny portion, numbering only in the thousands, of Florida's overall population of almost twenty million, yet these people have made a significant impact on the state's history and psyche. Since I have written this guide in the third person, let me take this opportunity to relay some personal experiences that contributed to my motivations for writing this book.

When I was a young man growing up in the Tallahassee area, I befriended an elderly gentleman named Jerry Carter. Jerry was from an old Tallahassee family and he relayed how his grandmother used to sing him a soothing lullaby when he was young. She said she learned the song as a little girl when she and her family were seeking refuge in the First Presbyterian Church—Tallahassee's oldest—during one of the Seminole scares during the Second Seminole War. Jerry sang a verse of the lullaby, and I regret that I don't remember it or didn't have a recorder, but I could easily visualize a large group of frightened women and children huddled in the church with only a few candles or oil lamps for light. Their men were standing guard along barricades on the town's edge, bonfires helping to alert them to unwelcome night intruders. The Florida frontier could be a dangerous place for American settlers. They faced a determined foe that resisted any forced removal from their home.

On another occasion, an elderly woman insisted that a Cherokee friend and I accompany her to some family property near Quincy, just west of Tallahassee, where a small spring had dried up after a logging company cleared the adjacent woods. She worried that the spring had been lost forever, but we presumed that seepage would eventually return when the adjacent land revegetated.

A grove of stately live oaks graced her property, the kind that had been growing for two or three hundred years or more. In seeing them, the old woman sighed and shared a family story.

"There was this old Indian man who stayed behind when his people were moved from this land," she began. "Maybe he was too old to make the trip, or maybe he hid, but he stayed and Grandma used to say she often saw him sitting against that live oak over there, smoking his pipe." She paused as if allowing the image its own time and space, an image that had lingered in her family's collective memory for more than a century and a half. I blinked and blinked again. I could easily visualize the elder still sitting there.

Gray hair flowed from beneath a plume-decorated turban. His shirt was faded gingham cloth, and he wore weathered deerskin moccasins. His pipe was made of fired clay, his tobacco home-grown and cut with native herbs. Sweet smelling.

During his time, I suspected that the man knew every bird and squirrel around the oak, even the ants that crawled over his skin. After sitting there for so long, maybe he felt like an extension of that tree, and the tree accepted him. Perhaps the oak, on that day at least, projected her phantom limb for me to see.

The woman, after finishing her short tale, turned to us, tears in her eyes, "It's so sad what we done to the Indians," she said. "I feel so ashamed."

Her outburst surprised me. We could only offer a sympathetic ear. So much guilt after so many years. I knew part of it was her family's connection with that specific ground, and with the elder.

Who was the elder? Surely, he was Muscogee Creek/Seminole, perhaps part of an area band led by Neamathla. Neamathla was the principal chief who signed the Treaty of Moultrie Creek in 1823 during which most of the Seminoles agreed to move to a reservation in Central Florida just south of present-day Ocala. Manifest Destiny was pushing the Seminoles deeper into the Florida peninsula. Only Neamathla's village and some small bands along the Apalachicola River could remain in their north Florida homes. But during the removals of the 1830s, America's Diaspora, Neamathla's band was marched to Montgomery, the men weighed down by iron manacles and chains. The 84-year-old Neamathla stoically lead the way "without uttering a complaint," according to one soldier. The *Montgomery Advertiser*, in a rare note of sympathy, wrote: "To see a remnant of a once-mighty people fettered and chained together forced to depart from the land of their fathers into a country unknown to them is ... sufficient to move the stoutest heart."

From Montgomery, the downtrodden band was loaded onto boats for the long trip to Indian Territory (now Oklahoma), minus one ancient warrior who slit his own throat just before embarkation. The "master race" would not have to worry about this band of Seminoles around Tallahassee any more.

But those are historic facts. What about emotions, feelings? What did the elder feel, the one left behind purposely or by accident? His whole world had been turned upside down; he lived his last days very differently than most of his forebears.

Where were his bones now resting?

More importantly, what can we do to honor his presence and his people today?

Over the years, I became involved with Muscogee Creek/Seminole descendants who observed traditional ceremonial ways in the Blountstown area. The late Seminole elder Mary Johns and her family were frequent visitors from the Brighton Seminole Reservation just above Lake Okeechobee. One evening, sitting around the sacred ceremonial fire, Mary relayed a story of how a Seminole band had been captured and were being held at Fort Brooke near Tampa. Shortly, they were to be put on a ship and taken to the western lands. They devised a plan of escape, and this is when tears began to form in Mary's eyes. "Some of the women agreed to offer themselves to the guards to distract them," she said, her voice lowering to a whisper. "They did this so their people could escape."

The sacrifices made during the Seminole wars were still being felt by Mary and her family, for this is why they were able to stay in Florida.

In exploring the Seminole Trail, maybe you'll have the opportunity to speak with someone with a long family history that extends back to the early Seminole experience. I urge you to grasp the Florida history that is represented here with more than your minds and with more than a camera click. Let these sites be like time machines to transport you to another era. This is the first step in healing the past and understanding the role of Seminole Indians in the place we call Florida.

Acknowledgments

I am sincerely grateful to the Seminole, Miccosukee, and Muscogee tribal members and various scholars and reenactors who shared with me during the research of this book. I especially want to acknowledge noted archaeologist and Muscogee leader Dan Penton for reviewing an early draft. He provided invaluable feedback and suggestions. Florida Seminole tribal chairman James Billie also offered encouragement and keen insights, something I deeply appreciated. Any mistakes that might remain are my own. I also want to thank June and David Cussen of Pineapple Press for their support in bringing this book to the general public. I hope many will follow The Great Florida Seminole Trail and find it as rewarding as I have.

One
Clearing the Way

The first stop on the Great Florida Seminole Trail is **Mission San Luis**, *a reconstruction of a Spanish mission for Apalachee Indians in downtown Tallahassee. Events here in 1704 helped to open up the region for later Seminole occupation.*

At first glance, Tallahassee's San Luis Mission Historical Site is an unlikely place to begin the Seminole Trail. First of all, the site's historical time period—1656 to 1704—preceded the mass migrations of Creek Indians from the north who, along with escaped slaves, would swell the population of Florida's Indians and form an amalgamation of people known as Seminoles. Before the Seminoles arrived, Apalachee Indians lived in north Florida with Spanish missionaries. They grew large amounts of corn to help feed the beleaguered Spanish city of St. Augustine.

When the English and their Creek Indian allies invaded in 1704, most Apalachee Indians were killed or dispersed, their former territory nearly completely denuded of people. Slowly, over the next few decades, Indians began to break away from the various Muscogee Creek bands to the north and resettle the land of the Apalachee, perhaps assimilating any Apalachee survivors still in the area. These Creek Indians settled the Apalachee capital of Anhaica and called it Tulwa-hassee, "Old Town" or "Old Fields" in acknowledgment of the former residents. They settled along rivers such as the Apalachicola, long used as trade routes for their predecessors, and they made frequent forays to the coast for seafood and items such as whelk shells. Eventually, they were called *simano-li* by their Creek brethren to the north, a term borrowed from the Spanish word *cimarron*, meaning "wild" or "runaway." Some linguists and historians postulate that the Creek definition also meant "separatist" or "those who camp at a distance."

The Seminoles had several years of relative peace, and their numbers swelled. And while they had contact with white traders, a handful of settlers, and Spanish and English government representatives, by and large they enjoyed a period of isolation. Unlike the Apalachee at Mission San Luis decades before.

In the early 1600s, with their population being decimated by European-introduced disease and threatened by enemies in all directions, the Apalachee chiefs invited Spanish Franciscan missionaries to their land between the Aucilla and Ochlockonee Rivers. Besides a need for security, perhaps the Apalachee equated Christianity and its prominent healer, Jesus, with the Spaniards' ability to ward off most of the diseases that were taking a toll on all of Florida's native populations. What the Spaniards gained was another foothold in the New World, their second largest after St. Augustine.

Today, in walking the grounds of San Luis and perusing the reconstructed Spanish and Apalachee buildings, you begin to grasp a large-

This reproduction Apalachee Council House at Mission San Luis in Tallahassee was similar in size and construction to council houses in Muscogee towns.

scale seventeenth century experiment in cultural exchange. A large plaza was set up with a church and priest quarters on one side and the chief's hut and an immense circular Apalachee council house on the other. Two traditional styles of architecture were at play—the Spanish waddle and daub and plank buildings, and the pole and thatch Apalachee structures.

The Apalachee council house could hold the entire adult San Luis Apalachee population of 1,400 plus guests. Other villages, along with those of nearby Creek Indians, had similar-sized council houses. To step inside the reconstructed building, with its sweet aroma of smoke and seasoned thatch, is almost dizzying. It is astonishing and worthy of Stonehenge comparisons to think these giant logs, weighing several tons each, were hoisted up by manual labor and handmade ropes.

The modern reconstruction was based on archaeological information and early Spanish descriptions and drawings. Old growth pines of approximately the same diameter as the originals were selectively harvested from private plantations and trucked in. Using cranes, they were leaned vertically to create a circular framework. Up to a million sabal palm fronds were thatched together for a covering. Log sitting platforms were built around an open hearth area where a large fire burned, the smoke funneling out the octagonal opening a hundred feet from the ground. One can sense the oratory that once occurred here, along with dances and other ceremonies.

The black drink—also used by Creeks and Seminoles—was often brewed ceremonially. This dark tea, made from roasted yaupon holly leaves, was the only Native American caffeinated drink in the Southeast and it was often used as a purgative, thus the Latin name *Ilex vomitoria*. Even though most Apalachee willingly adopted Christianity, they still retained many of their traditional beliefs and customs. Besides the black drink, another example was the ball game.

Spanish priests frowned upon the sometimes violent ball game in which players tried to kick a small leather ball at a pole or into a reconstructed eagle's nest on top of the pole. Tackling was the norm and the Apalachees played it with gusto. They gambled corn, jewelry, and other items on the outcome, just like Creek and Seminole Indians with their lacrosse-style stickball game, which was often called "the little brother of war." The entire community participated in pregame ceremonies, such as the raising of the ballpost. "It was their greatest festival," Friar Juan de Paiva wrote in 1676. And because some of the ball game ceremonies had religious overtones, he characterized the pole as "this ballpost of the devil." The game and ballpost were associated with rain and thunder, a necessity for good crops. Interestingly, the Friar claimed the ballposts were hit by lightning and burned to the ground on several occasions.

Friar Paiva sought to make a case against the ball game to have it banned, so he made detailed observations on how it was played. Contemporary scholars wish there had been other controversial aspects of traditional Apalachee beliefs and ceremonies that warranted such attention, but Friar Paiva's vivid description of the Apalachee ball game is the most detailed account that has survived. Here is part of his account, as translated in John Hann's *Apalachee, the Land Between the Rivers*:

> They all crowd together like a clump of pine-cones, naked as when their mother bore them, except for a deerskin breechclout that covers their private parts, and, [with] their hair braided. And a leading man throws the ball in the midst of all of them, who are erect and with their hands raised. It falls into the hand of someone. And they fall upon one another at full tilt. And the last to arrive climb up over their bodies, using them as stairs. And, to enter, others [step on] their faces, heads, or bellies, as they encounter them, taking no notice [of them] and aiming kicks without any concern whether it is to the face or to the body, while in other places still others pull at arms or legs with no concern as to whether they may be dislocated or not, while still others have their mouths filled with dirt. When this pileup begins to become untangled, they are accustomed to find four or five stretched out like tuna; over there are others gasping for breath, because, inasmuch as some are wont to swallow the ball, they are made to vomit it up by squeezing their windpipe or by kicks to the stomach. Over there lie others with an arm or

leg broken. … How can these wretches stay alive thus? Accordingly, they are destroying themselves and this nation is being extinguished. And all this is only a sketch.

Attempts to ban the ball game ultimately succeeded. It would be similar to priests and ministers and the pope himself weaning modern society from participating in or watching tackle football on grounds that it was too violent and that it promoted debauchery.

So what did the Apalachee gain from these meddling Spaniards? For one, they achieved some level of protection. The site of San Luis was chosen because it was a hilltop that afforded a broad view of the region, and so a Spanish fort manned by a garrison was built near the mission site. But a heavy price was paid for this security. The rich Apalachee lands were increasingly used to raise food for the struggling city of St. Augustine, a population center that experienced chronic food shortages. Apalachee men were forced to leave their families and carry corn and other foods by foot to the city. Non-Christian Apalachee rebelled in 1647 and were brutally subdued. The intercultural experiment wasn't always peaceful.

In 1676, a 33-year Spanish veteran of the Florida missions, Fray Alonso Moral, provided a graphic portrayal of how Apalachee laborers were forced to carry heavy loads on their backs for two hundred miles to and from St. Augustine: "Each year from Apalachee alone more than three hundred are brought to the fort [in St. Augustine] at the time of the planting of the corn, carrying their food and the merchandise of the soldiers on their shoulders for more than eighty leagues with the result that some on arrival die and this without paying them a wage… This is the reason according to the commonly held opinion that they are being annihilated at such a rate." The brutal work and poor conditions weakened the workers and left them vulnerable to diseases.

The Mission San Luis era ended abruptly in 1704. British Governor

James Moore of South Carolina, himself a Christian but not Spanish or Catholic, put together a force of fifty whites and more than a thousand Creek allies and swept into the land of the Apalachee. All fourteen mission villages and numerous satellite settlements and Spanish ranches between the Aucilla and Ochlockonee Rivers were burned and their inhabitants either killed, enslaved, or forced into exile. Many of the Apalachee groups who dispersed were eventually hunted down, with the exception of those who fled west with the Spanish to Pensacola and Mobile. The land of Apalachee, once considered the most concentrated native population in the state, numbering around 8,000, lay in ruins.

The only known people who identify themselves as Apalachee today live near Lubuse, Louisiana. They had largely kept below the radar for nearly three centuries until tribal members, using parish records, discovered their link to San Luis. For decades, scholars such as veteran San Luis archaeologist Bonnie McEwan had thought the tribe was extinct. But then, in March of 1996, Dr. McEwan received a call: "This is Gilmer Bennett, chief of the Apalachee." History suddenly came alive, giving increased relevancy and a human face to her research at San Luis.

Bennett had served as chief of the Tamali Band of Apalachee since 1954 and the group of about 150 has been seeking federal recognition since 1997. Times were never easy since their Florida exodus. After the British invasion, they fled with the Spanish to Mobile, but yellow fever decimated ninety percent of the survivors, reducing the population from 800 to about 80. They moved to Louisiana in the early 1800s and settled along the Red River, but American settlers soon began burning their homes and seizing their fertile farm land. They were forced to flee to marginal lands in Louisiana's bayou and hill country where they were eventually subjected to Jim Crow laws for being dark-skinned. They have been struggling ever since, but no longer do the remaining Apalachee seek to hide their heritage from the outside world. Tribal members make periodic visits to San Luis in a type of modern-day pilgrimage. Perhaps the grand experiment is not over, and we still have something to learn from each other.

So what about the Seminoles? With the Apalachees decimated, their old homeland was so denuded of people that a Spanish visitor in 1716 noted how once uncommon bison now inhabited the vacant San Luis region. This human population void would eventually be filled by Creek Indians from northern regions who spoke either Muscogee or Hitchiti. Their reasons for migrating into Florida were opportunity, safety, and debt.

In the mid to late 1700s, the deer skin trade was in full swing, driven by an Indian desire for European trade goods such as guns, iron kettles, and tomahawks. British traders inhabited nearly every village, and they kept a tally of what was owed. The Indians were nearly always behind. For example, by 1711, the amount of debt owed by the Ocheese Creeks of central Georgia amounted to a shocking 100,000 deerskins. "They wage eternal war against deer and bear, to procure food and cloathing [sic], and other necessaries and conveniences; which is indeed carried to an unreasonable and perhaps criminal excess, since the white people have dazzled their senses with foreign superfluities," concluded William Bartram in 1774. It was a pattern of debt with which many modern Americans can certainly relate.

Deer were becoming scarce as a result, and so Indian hunters had to travel weeks and even months away from home to find enough deer to pay their debts. Florida offered a fertile hunting ground. Over time, hunters grew tired of the long forays, and so a few brought their families and established new villages.

The Yamassee War of 1715 to 1717, one in which several Lower Creek tribes failed in their attempts to push the British out of South Carolina, was also a factor in the Florida migration. Indian participants feared retribution, and the Florida frontier was a convenient hideout. This scenario would be repeated in 1814 when survivors of the failed

Red Stick War fled south, and generations of escaped slaves would also find refuge in Florida among the Seminoles.

So, during the early to mid 1700s, not only was old Apalachee reoccupied by native people, but Creeks moved into the Alachua savannah country of current-day Paynes Prairie, into the upper Florida East Coast along the St. Johns River, and along the Suwannee River, perhaps merging with remnant bands of other Florida tribes. They retained many of the customs and beliefs of their Muscogee relatives to the north, but the geographic separation eventually caused political divisions, especially when Indian bands were being pressured to side with Americans or different European powers.

So how did those Seminoles evolve and what was the cultural and material exchange between cultures? Let us continue down the Seminole Trail and find out.

Native American interpreter Tammy Lee-Lannigan in reconstructed Apalachee Council House at Mission San Luis in Tallahassee.

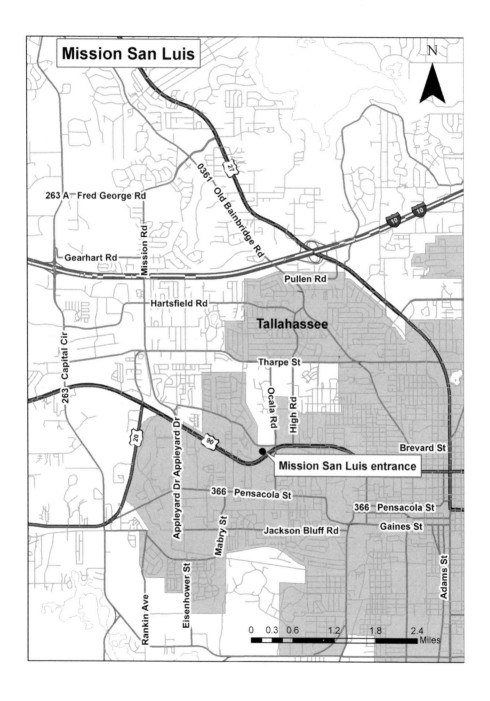

Getting There

Mission San Luis is open from 10 a.m. to 4 p.m. Tuesday through Sunday. It is closed on most major holidays. Visitors can see several reconstructed historic buildings, including the Apalachee council house, Franciscan church, the Franciscan friary, the home of the Spanish deputy governor, Spanish fort and blockhouse, a traditional garden, and a blacksmith's workshop. The visitor's center displays historical items found on the site along with realistic oil paintings of mission life by Charles F. Manning.

The site is accessed from Highway 90, the main east-west thoroughfare through Tallahassee. The highway can easily be reached by travelers on I-10 by taking the FL 263/Capital Circle Northwest exit 196 towards the regional airport. Travel about a mile south and take a left onto Highway 90/West Tennessee Street. The mission entrance is about three miles on the left. A city bus also stops nearby.

Mission San Luis has frequent events, educational programs, and youth camps. Larger events include a traditional Franciscan blessing of the animals, a Thanksgiving festival, and a commemorative mass. Call 850-245-6406 for more information or check their website, http://www. missionsanluis.org/visitorInfo/index.cfm. The address is 2100 W. Tennessee St., Tallahassee, FL 32304-1624.

Two

The Alachua Savanna

*The Seminole Trail continues to **Paynes Prairie Preserve State Park** near Gainesville, a.k.a. the Alachua Savannah. In the mid-1700s, a large body of Creek Indians left Georgia to settle along the vast savannahs. They soon became known as Seminoles.*

The deerskin trade and the lure of land largely uninhabited by whites prompted the Oconee Creek Chief *Ahaya* to move to the Alachua Savannah country from central Georgia around 1750. He set up a village on the south side of the Alachua Prairie—what is now called Paynes Prairie just south of present-day Gainesville—possibly near the site of the once-prosperous Timucuan village of Potano. The land consisted of rich hardwood forests, fertile soil, abundant game, lakes full of fish, and herds of wild cattle descended from Spanish stock. These new Florida inhabitants built pens and rounded up the cattle, which earned *Ahaya* the name Cowkeeper. His band was perhaps the best documented group of early Seminoles.

Paynes Prairie, a.k.a. the Alachua Savannah, near Gainesville.

Before proceeding further, it should be noted that historians and tribal members of the Seminole Tribe of Florida differ with or expand upon widespread theories concerning Seminole origins. They assert that members of the Seminole Tribe of Florida not only share genes with Muscogee people who were originally north of the Florida border, but also early Florida and Caribbean aboriginal tribes as well as Africans, Spanish, French, and British. They maintain that at the time of the Muscogee migration into Florida in the 1700s and early 1800s, there were still scattered groups of native people already living in Florida who survived European diseases and persecution and that many of these people eventually amalgamated with the new arrivals for their common survival. Thus, the tribe claims continuous habitation of Florida and the Southeast for more than 12,000 years. "Creek, Hitchiti, Apalachee, Mikisuki,

Yamassee, Yuchic, Tequesta, Apalachicola, Choctaw, and Oconee were joined by escaped slaves and others in the pursuit of better lives among the thick virgin forests, wide grass prairies and spring-fed rivers of interior Florida," the Seminole Tribe of Florida website summarizes. "They shared an instinct for survival and a commonality of purpose: refusal to be dominated by the white man."

What is largely agreed upon is that there was a band of Oconee Creeks who migrated into the Alachua Prairie country in the mid-1700s, and their leader was known as Cowkeeper.

At first, Cowkeeper's village was conveniently perched on the edge of the Alachua Savannah since the great prairie had filled with water and was now a lake teeming with fish. But after fifteen years, the lake dried and the stench of rotting fish became so great that the village was moved farther south to where the town of Micanopy now sits. This new village was called Cuscowilla.

Cowkeeper had no great love for the Spanish and he claimed to have received a visionary instruction to kill one hundred Spaniards in his lifetime. To fulfill this directive, Cowkeeper waged war on the Spanish and on any Florida Indians allied with them. In 1763, after the French and Indian War, Spain ceded St. Augustine to the British since Spain had been allied with France. During negotiations with the British, the Oconees' desire to be treated as an independent tribe from other Creeks to the north earned them the name *Semanoles* or Seminoles, a name which was first documented in 1765.

In 1774, since there was relative peace under British rule, a trading company laid out an ambitious plan to set up trading posts near Cowkeeper's village of Cuscowilla and on the Suwannee River near the village of Talahasochte, just north of present-day Manatee Springs State Park. One expedition included a 34-year-old naturalist named William Bartram.

Bartram had, in the words of one admirer, "that rarest of combinations—the mind of a scientist with the soul of a poet." He wrote extensively about the plants, animals and terrain of wild Florida, but he also wrote with a sympathetic flair about the Seminole Indians, with whom he spent a considerable amount of time. They show "the most striking picture of happiness in this life; joy, contentment, love and friendship, without guile or affectation," Bartram wrote. Of Cowkeeper, Bartram added, "The chief is a tall well made man, very affable and cheerful, about sixty years of age, his eyes lively and full of fire, his countenance manly and placid, yet ferocious, or what we call savage; his nose aquiline, his dress extremely simple, but his head trimmed and ornamented in the true Creek mode."

Bartram described Cuscowilla as having a large cleared square in the center surrounded by about thirty family camps, each with two log houses about 30 feet in length and 12 feet wide. One house would be divided into two rooms—a kitchen and a common hall—and the other house was two stories tall and divided into sections for lodging and for storing food. Some houses had a raised open-sided platform for the head of the household to rest in hot seasons and to entertain visitors. Roofs were covered with cypress bark. A small garden plot at each camp grew corn, beans, squash, tobacco and citrus, while broader farms and grazing areas stretched along the great savannah. "Their towns are clean, the inhabitants being particular in laying their filth at a proper distance from their dwellings, which undoubtedly contributes to the healthiness of their habitations," Bartram observed.

Protecting the village's large farms was the responsibility of boys by day and men by night.

> The youth, under the supervisal of some of their ancient people, are daily stationed in their fields, who are continually whooping and hallooing, to chase away crows, jackdaws, black-birds and such predatory animals, and the lads are armed with bows and arrows, who, being

trained up to it from their early youth, are sure at a mark, and in the course of the day load themselves with squirrels, birds, &c. The men in turn patrole the Corn fields at night, to protect their provisions from the depredations of night rovers, as bears, raccoons and deer; the two former being immoderately fond of young Corn, when the grain is filled with a rich milk, as sweet and nourishing as cream, and the deer are as fond of the Potatoe vines.

Of the natural world, Bartram first described the black or red wolf as well as 125 new plant species and many animal varieties. His curiosity of the natural world earned him a name among the Seminoles—*Puc Puggy*, (the Flower Hunter). The Muscogee pronunciation of his name is *buck-ba-gee*, which has dual meanings besides flower—the foam (or blossom) on liquid plant medicine after it is doctored, and semen. Bartram was given "unlimited permission to travel over the country for the purpose of collecting flowers, medicinal plants, etc.," according to his journal.

The Seminoles were certainly botanists and naturalists in their own right, having developed hundreds of uses for various herbs and plants. Even in the twentieth century, after the Seminoles were driven into South Florida, some Seminole medicine people retained knowledge of plants found only in north Florida. It was one motivation for Seminoles to accept invitations to the Florida Folk Festival in White Springs along the Suwannee River. Ginseng *(hillis hvtke)*, for example—now very rare in the wilds due to high demand in Asia—is found only in the deep north Florida woods. It is used for pain, shortness of breath, heart disease, and by ceremonial leaders for clarity and energy.

William Sturtevant lists about 225 medicinal herbs known by the famous twentieth-century medicine man Josie Billie, having interviewed him from 1950 to 1952. Alice Snow, co-author of *Healing Plants: Medicine of the Florida Seminole Indians*, cited 74 medicine plants she used. In one study in the mid-1990s, eight elderly women on the Brighton Reservation remembered about two hundred different herbs. Most frequently mentioned were *tolv* (red bay) and *passv* (button snakeroot). Also mentioned were wax myrtle, huckleberry, blue flag or iris, elderberry, button snakeroot, ginseng, goldenrod, mallow, maple, penny royal, sage, sassafras, saw palmetto, sumac, sundew, and willow.

One fascinating account written by Bartram in 1774 involves the rattlesnake or *jetto mekko*—"king of snakes." He was staying with a group of Seminoles when he was alerted about a very large rattlesnake crawling through the camp: ". . . the dreaded and revered serpent leisurely traversed their camp, visiting the fireplaces from one to another, picking up fragments of their provisions, and licking their platters." His new friends entreated him to help, whereupon Bartram dispatched the snake, much to their appreciation. Soon afterwards, a group of Seminole men approached him in order to ceremonially scratch him with sharp garfish teeth to alleviate any bad medicine that he brought upon himself for killing the snake. "These people never kill the rattle snake or any other serpent," Bartram explained, "saying if they do so, the spirit of the killed snake will excite or influence his living kindred or relatives to revenge the injury or violence done to him when alive."

It is unknown whether Bartram was ever told the Muscogee story of the rattlesnake woman, a mythological and irresistible being who periodically came to the annual Green Corn ceremonies to claim a new mate. As a result, there was a belief among the people that they might be related to rattlesnakes, thus the reason for not killing any of the venomous serpents, even when they crawled through their villages and dwellings.

Bartram also journeyed to the Seminole village of Talahasochte along the Little St. Juan River, now called the Suwannee River, three or four miles north of Manatee Spring on an elevated east bank. The young naturalist was astounded at the large cypress dugout canoes capable of seating twenty or thirty occupants that the Indians used for long trade journeys downstream to the Gulf of Mexico and from there, to the Caribbean. "In these large canoes they descend the river on trading and hunting expeditions to the sea coast, neighboring islands and keys, quite to the point of Florida, and sometimes cross the gulph, extending their navigations to the Bahama islands, and even to Cuba; a crew of these adventurers had just arrived, having returned from Cuba but a few days before our arrival, with a cargo of spirituous liquors, Coffee, Sugar, and Tobacco. One of them politely presented me with a choice piece of Tobacco, which he told me he had received from the governor of Cuba."

In return for the Spanish goods, Bartram reported that the Seminoles traded deerskins, furs, dried fish, beeswax, honey, bear's oil, and other articles.

While some Americans, such as William Bartram, merely wanted to explore the lands of the Southeast and try to learn more from its native inhabitants, many other Americans aggressively sought to possess the land and drive the Indians away. Chief among them was John Bryan of Georgia, who tricked Creek chiefs in Georgia on two occasions into signing over millions of acres on the ruse that he merely wanted to set up a trading post.

In 1783, Britain turned control of Florida back to Spain after losing the Revolutionary War. Cowkeeper died that year and his son, Payne, took over. Paynes Prairie, what Bartram had called the Alachua Savannah, was named after this Seminole chief. Payne moved his village just west of present-day Micanopy and called it Paynestown. Before Cowkeeper's death, Payne was enjoined by the old chief to finish fulfilling his vision of killing one hundred Spaniards. It is unclear whether Payne killed the 14 Spaniards required to reach his father's goal.

In the late 1700s, escaped black slaves began to form a strong alliance with the Seminoles, emulating a similar alliance they had established with the Spanish that resulted in the creation of Fort Mose near St. Augustine. Together, the blacks and Seminoles represented a formidable front against their mutual enemy, the Americans. The blacks set up their own villages near their Seminole compatriots along Paynes Prairie. As a result, white slave owners to the north became increasingly outraged and alarmed.

On Sept 24, 1812, Payne and nearly a hundred of his warriors left on a trail to the northeast to visit St. Augustine. After only a few miles, at Lake Pithlachocco (later named Newnan's Lake by settlers), they were met with hostile gunfire by 117 American militia troops led by Colonel Daniel Newnan. Weary of border skirmishes, the Georgia governor had sent Newnan to destroy the Alachua Seminoles, capture escaped slaves, and gain control of Florida. The American government unofficially supported this group of Florida and Georgia militia, part of the Patriot Rebellion, in hopes they would seize control of this section of Florida and cede it to the United States government. In return, the volunteer soldiers were promised captured slaves and free land for homesteading.

These "Patriot Rebels" had a running battle with the Seminoles, and Payne, at eighty years old, was wounded in the leg. The Seminoles retreated to a swamp and Newnan erected a log breastwork. The standoff lasted the rest of the day. Word of the fighting spread and soon the Seminoles doubled their ranks, partly with black allies. The soldiers became entrapped in their breastworks for seven days, a foreshadowing of later battles that occurred along the Withlacoochee River during the Second Seminole War. Newnan sent a messenger north with a desperate plea: "I am now entrenched within six miles of the nation and must sacrifice the sick and wounded or perish for the want of provisions, unless you send me a reinforcement immediately. We commence eating horses tonight." When only four horses remained, the Seminoles shot them so the soldiers couldn't save them for food since they had no way to preserve the meat.

Eventually, Newnan and his troops retreated under the constant harassment of Seminole gunfire. On their way north, the troops survived on gopher tortoises, alligators, and palmetto buds until reinforcements arrived. Newnan lost sixteen men and many more were wounded. They scalped several of the Seminoles they had killed.

After the battle, fearing retaliation, Payne moved his village south. His brother, Bowlegs, moved to the lower Suwannee River near present-day Old Town. Two months later, Payne died of his wound, but his decision to move the village proved to be a wise one. Five months later, 250 Tennessee volunteers attacked the Alachua area. Some other migrating Indians—mostly women and old men—had settled in the abandoned villages; the volunteers killed sixty of them. In their swing through East Florida, the volunteers burned 386 Indian dwellings, destroyed 1,500 to 2,000 bushels of corn, and drove off herds of Seminole horses and cattle. Temporarily, the Seminole strength in the area had been broken, and the remaining Indians were deprived of valuable food stocks.

About a year later, a former Georgia slaver named Buckner Harris built a blockhouse for his 160 men near Payne's former village and proclaimed the area to be "The District of Elotchaway of the Republic of East Florida." On May 5, 1814, while Harris was out surveying his new empire, he was killed by a scouting party of Seminole and black warriors. The new republic soon collapsed. The rest of The Patriot Rebellion had dissolved as well. While patriot forces had easily captured the coastal village of Fernandina, they failed to breach the coquina walls of Castillo de San Marcos in St. Augustine. However, the idea of claiming Florida for the United States stayed alive, and many former patriot soldiers remained in Florida.

With Payne's death, Bowlegs became the hereditary chief of the Alachua Seminoles. He joined the British in 1814 at the Battle of New Orleans, whereupon he made a bitter enemy, one who would feature prominently in future events involving the Seminoles—Andrew Jackson. Paynes Prairie would also be the site of conflict during the Second Seminole War, most notably on December 18, 1835, when Osceola and 81 warriors ambushed a baggage train. This was followed by a skirmish with the local militia in which the Seminoles killed six and wounded eight—the Battle of Black Point—one of several incidents that marked the beginning of a seven-year war. The relatively peaceful days of Cowkeeper and Cuscowilla along the Alachua Savannah were no more.

Getting There

The 21,000-acre Paynes Prairie Preserve State Park features several trails and a viewing tower of the vast savannah enjoyed by early Seminole inhabitants. The park features both bison herds and scrub cattle—descendants of the Spanish herds raised by Seminoles—along with 400 other species of vertebrates and more than 800 species of plants.

The park's visitor's center, open 9 a.m. to 4 p.m. daily, features several exhibits and an audio-visual program of the natural and cultural history of the area. Park hours are 8 a.m. until sunset 365 days a year. Camping is available. The address for Paynes Prairie Preserve State Park is 100 Savannah Blvd., Micanopy, FL 32667; (352) 466-3397. The park can be reached along Highway 441 just south of Gainesville. Interstate 75 also traverses the prairie, and a rest area on the northern border provides a broad view.

The town of Micanopy, less than five miles south of the state park just off U.S. 441, is a charming village of restaurants and antique shops. A sign in the oak-canopied town square describes Bartram's visit and the Seminole town of Cuscowilla. While in Micanopy, be sure to visit the Micanopy Historical Society Museum and Archives. There are several exhibits relating to the Seminoles and the Second Seminole War. The museum is open from 1 to 4 p.m. daily. The address is 607 NE First Street, Cholokka Blvd. at Bay Street, Micanopy, 32667; (352) 466-3200.

Newnan's Lake, what the Seminoles called Lake Pithlachocco

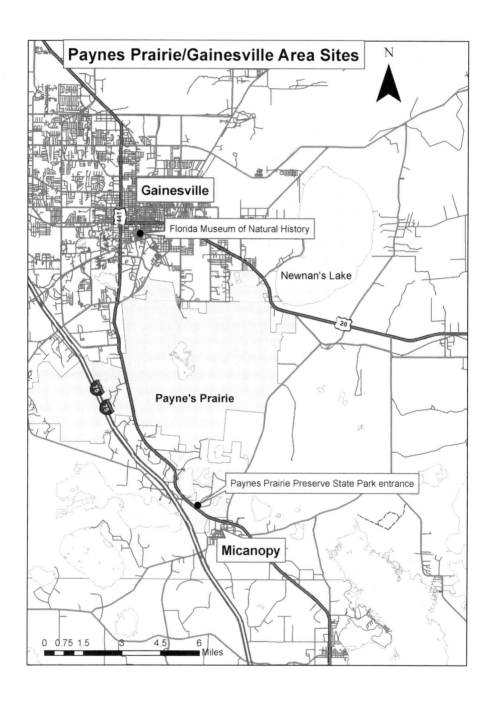

Paynes Prairie/Gainesville Area Sites

N

Gainesville

Florida Museum of Natural History

Newnan's Lake

Payne's Prairie

Paynes Prairie Preserve State Park entrance

Micanopy

0 0.75 1.5   3   4.5   6
                              Miles

Downtown Micanopy near the site of the Seminole village of Cuscowilla.

("Boat House"), can be accessed at several public parks and landings just east of Gainesville. In the year 2000, during a prolonged drought, more than a hundred dugout canoes were discovered in the lake bottom, the largest cache of Native American canoes in North America. The lake bottom is now part of the National Register of Historic Places, and the Seminole Tribe of Florida played an active role in its protection.

Manatee Springs State Park, just south of the Seminole village of Talahasochte on the Suwannee River, can be reached by driving to Chiefland on Highway 19 and following the signs. The address is 11650 N.W. 115th Street, Chiefland, Florida 32626; (352) 493-6072.

While in the Gainesville area, don't miss the Florida Museum of

Natural History, which features several Seminole-related exhibits. Hours are 10 a.m. to 5 p.m. Monday through Saturday, and Sunday from 1 to 5 p.m. They are open every day of the year except for Thanksgiving and Christmas. From I-75, take exit 384 (State Road 24) and follow the signs. From U.S. 441, travel two miles west of State Road 24, turn north (right) on State Road 121 (SW 34th St), and turn right onto Hull Road at the third traffic light. The museum is part of the University of Florida Cultural Plaza on the south side of Hull Road. The address is SW 34th Street and Hull Road, Gainesville, FL 32611-2710; (352) 846-2000. Admission to the main part of the museum is free.

Three
Dreams of Freedom

From the Alachua Savannah, the Seminole Trail loops back to north Florida and the lower Apalachicola River, where many free blacks, escaped slaves and Seminoles occupied a former British Fort in the early 1800s. The initial battle for the fort and region served as a prelude to the First Seminole War. The site is currently known as the **Fort Gadsden Historical Site** *in the Apalachicola National Forest.*

"The Negro Fort ... has been strengthened ... and is now occupied by between two hundred and fifty and three hundred blacks, who are well armed, clothed, and disciplined. Secret practices to inveigle negroes from the frontiers of Georgia, as well as from the Cherokee and Creek nations, are still continued by the negroes and hostile Creeks. This is a state of things which cannot fail to produce much injury to the neighboring settlements, and excite irritations which may ultimately endanger the peace of the nation." — Secretary of War William Crawford, 1816

reedom. Hope. These feelings were prevalent at Negro Fort along the lower Apalachicola River. Several hundred free blacks, escaped slaves, and Seminole Indians took over an abandoned English fort in 1814 in hopes of defending their domain. Spain had reclaimed La Florida from the English in 1783, but they held most of the territory in name only, focusing more on their military garrisons at Pensacola, St. Marks, and St. Augustine. The interior ramparts were left to Seminoles, blacks, British agents and traders, and a few adventuresome Americans.

Spain disliked the English during the European colonization of the New World. They were competitors and they had often battled, especially on the high seas. But in regards to Florida after the American Revolution, the Spanish saw a need to retain the goodwill of Creeks and Seminoles as a buffer against American encroachment. And since the Indians could get good quality English trade goods for a better price, the Spanish allowed the British firm Panton, Leslie and Company to establish a virtual trade monopoly in Spanish Florida. The firm built stores along the St. Johns River, in Pensacola, on the Wakulla River four miles north of the St. Marks River confluence, and on the lower Apalachicola River at Prospect Bluff. During the War of 1812, the British built a fort at the Prospect Bluff trading post site, and when they abandoned it after the war's conclusion, they turned it over—fully armed with cannon, powder, and guns—to a large group of free blacks, escaped slaves, and a few Indians. It would be called Negro Fort.

Negro Fort and the surrounding area became a beacon for Indians retreating from white expansion in Alabama and Georgia, especially after their failed efforts in the Red Stick War and the Battle of Horseshoe Bend in 1814. About one thousand Red Stick warriors fled to Florida.

For slaves in the Deep South, Florida, especially Negro Fort, was a closer haven than states north of the Mason Dixon Line, and as many as eight hundred may have heeded the call. Naturally, slave owners were upset. An alliance of blacks and Indians with England threatened the plantation way of life and stood in the way of expansionist dreams. Plus, with the annihilation of the Creeks during the Red Stick War, whereupon Andrew Jackson extracted more than twenty million acres from them in Alabama and Georgia, white settlers had gained new confidence that they could push through any Indian—or Negro—obstacle.

In 1814 and 1815, slave hunters made constant forays into Florida. Seminoles and blacks responded by raiding settlements and plantations north of the Florida/Georgia border. During this period, the United States government built Fort Scott along the Georgia border where the Chattahoochee and Flint Rivers formed the Apalachicola River. The idea was for Fort Scott to be a supply depot for American bases in New Orleans via the river and Gulf Coast, but Negro Fort stood in the way. "I have very little doubt of the fact that this fort [Negro Fort] has been established by some villains for the purpose of murder, rapine, and plunder," wrote General Andrew Jackson to General Edmund P. Gaines in 1816, "and that it ought to be blown up regardless of the ground it stands on."

Even though the fort lay in Spanish Florida, a raid was planned, the objective of which was to "capture the negroes within the fort, and restore them to their proper owners," according to Colonel Duncan Clinch.

In July of 1816, an army of almost three hundred American soldiers and Creek allies appeared on land at Negro Fort, led by Colonel Clinch. The invaders demanded the fort's surrender. But the black warriors inside preferred to die than be forced back into slavery, and the Indians were tired of running. Without warning, one of the fort's cannons spewed fire. A whistle and roar filled the air. It was the fort's defiant answer. The battle for Negro Fort had begun.

While the ground battle raged, American warships sailed upriver. Soon, a cannon battle erupted between the fort and ships. Blasts from ships slammed into the fort's dirt breastworks. The fort's cannons hurled shells into the water around the ships. Waterspouts shot up several feet. Smoke grew thick, often obstructing the view. The fort's thick walls held up well and none of the ships were hurt either. "We were pleased with their spirited opposition," wrote surgeon Marcus Buck afterwards, "though they were Indians, negroes and our enemies."

After several more volleys, the experienced sailors in the ships, having found the range they desired, began to heat up cannonballs in cook stoves. One of the ships then shot a red hot cannonball that sailed over the fort's walls. There was a brief flash. Suddenly, the earth rocked and shook as the cannonball ignited several hundred casks of stored gunpowder in the fort's main magazine. Negro Fort disintegrated in a colossal explosion. Bodies, burning logs, and bright tongues of flame flew in all directions.

"The explosion was awful and the scene horrible beyond description," reported Colonel Clinch afterwards. "The Great Ruler of the Universe must have used us as his instruments in chastising the blood-thirsty and murderous wretches that defended the fort."

Marcus Buck added, in a letter to his father, "You cannot conceive, nor I describe the horrors of the scene. In an instant, hundreds of life-less bodies were stretched upon the plain, buried in sand and rubbish, or suspended from the tops of surrounding pines. ... Here lay an innocent babe, there a helpless mother, on the other side a sturdy warrior, on the other a bleeding squaw. ... The brave soldier was disarmed of his resentment, and checked his victorious career, to drop a tear on the distressing scene." The blast was reportedly heard in Pensacola, more than a hundred miles away. It was perhaps the single most significant cannon shot in early American history.

Of the 320 men, women, and children in the fort, 270 died instantly from the blast. Most of the survivors were badly wounded, and the fort's leader, Garcon, was executed along with a surviving Choctaw chief. Other blacks were marched north to Fort Scott and put back into slavery.

As payment for their services, McIntosh's Creeks were allowed to plunder most of the surviving military supplies of the fort, including

Artist's rendering at the Fort Gadsden Historic site museum of the Negro Fort explosion.

2,500 British muskets, 50 carbines, 500 swords, nearly 400 pistols, and numerous barrels and kegs of gunpowder that survived the explosion. It was enough to equip a small army. The United States military leaders took most of the artillery pieces.

Less than two years later, during his march through north Florida that became the First Seminole War, General Andrew Jackson ordered Lieutenant James Gadsden to rebuild the destroyed Negro Fort on Prospect Bluff. Gadsden completed the job in just ten days. Jackson was so impressed that he ordered the new fort to bear Gadsden's name. Gadsden County also honors the young lieutenant. The fort was later fortified with more substantial timbers, and extensive earthworks were developed. The fort was used as a garrison post until 1821 when Spain ceded Florida to the United States, whereupon the fort was abandoned and the troops were transferred to the fort at St. Marks.

The site of Negro Fort was and still is remote. Once accessible by river and Indian trails, access today is by back highways and forest roads and also by river. The nearest town is Sumatra, population 11. Ironically, fewer people live in the area now than in 1815. Then, sizeable villages thrived along the river and near the fort.

A pleasant drive to the historic fort site is through second-growth longleaf pine forests that are beginning to resemble their old-growth forebears. Here, you'll see banded pines marking the nest cavity trees of the red-cockaded woodpecker, the only woodpecker that pecks a cavity home in a living tree. The Apalachicola National Forest harbors the largest concentration of these endangered birds in the world, just one of a vast array of species that were here when Seminoles roamed these parts. And with the exception of panthers, wolves, bison, Carolina parakeets, passenger pigeons, and ivory-billed woodpeckers, a large cornucopia of species still exists in the forest.

Travel the roads in fall and spring and you'll be treated to flowering meadows and roadsides. Colorful blazing star, deer tongue, and aster fill the forest with color in fall while springtime offers up blooming pitcher plants, grass pink orchids, and coreopsis. Bring along a wildflower identification guide. You won't be disappointed.

For the scenic tour, take Highway 12 heading southwest off Highway 65 at Wilma. This back road skirts more of the unique wet prairies amid the piney woods. Frequent fire and a hardpan of clay keep these meadows treeless, and many of the cypress trees that grow along the creek strands are stunted. An interesting side trip is to the dwarf cypress forest in Tate's Hell Swamp southeast of Sumatra. Accessed from Highway 65 as well, these miniature old-growth trees likely fascinated people for thousands of years, perhaps the ideal home for dwarflike spiritual beings the Seminoles and Creeks referred to as the *isti-lah-bugs-chee* or *stee-la-booch-go-gee*, "the little people."

At the Fort Gadsden Historic Site, five enclosed kiosks with artifacts tell the story of Negro Fort and Fort Gadsden. You can hike to the cleared fort area and view the moat and breastworks dug two centuries before. An American flag flies near the river where Fort Gadsden stood, while a British flag near the rear of the site marks the spot where the fort's magazine stood before being ignited by the red hot cannonball.

A trail behind the fort site winds through an unspoiled longleaf forest, the understory dominated by native wiregrass and gallberry, sunflower, and palmetto. Just as you become enraptured by the beauty of this nature trail, you come across a small clearing of shallow depressions. This is the "Renegade Graveyard" where many of those killed in the Negro Fort explosion were buried. The realization of the spot's significance is brought home. For many who came here seeking refuge

Fort Gadsden historic display.

31

and to start a new life, even to establish a new country where blacks and Indians could live in relative peace, this was the last stop.

Grave robbers in the early 1900s broke into a red brick burial vault of the Renegade Graveyard, but there wasn't much to find. Acidic soil had destroyed most of the physical remains, and the Negro Fort occupants didn't possess a wealth of material goods. What was of value at the time was likely stripped by their attackers. But hope did not completely die here. Seminoles and blacks in the region who were not killed fled east to other villages, or they stealthily withdrew into the woods and returned to rebuild their villages after the invaders left. One raid—or cannonball—could not destroy the Seminole spirit.

A year and a half later, on November 30, 1817, a force of Seminole, Creek, and black warriors—sparked by the U.S. Army attack on the Creek village of Fowltown along the Georgia border a few days before—attacked a boatload of Americans heading up the Apalachicola River near present-day Chattahoochee. The boat's leader, Lieutenant Richard W. Scott, had been warned about the gathering of hostile Indians, but proceeded anyway. Forty-one men, six women, and four children were killed in the attack, helping to foment a furor that would lead to the First Seminole War. The site of the raid was just below the Apalachicola River landing in Chattahoochee on the east side of the river where numerous military artifacts from the era have been found.

While news of the Scott boat raid raged across newspapers of a young country soon after it occurred, word of the 1816 raid on Negro Fort in Spanish Florida would not be known by the general public until 1837, when Congressman William Jay broke the story. Perhaps it was because Negro Fort stood on land claimed by Spain at the time, or because it was as much a slave raid as it was a punitive action against the Seminoles.

The raid on the fort and other actions of the First Seminole War were used as examples to justify abolitionist arguments in the 1850s,

Site of Fort Gadsden today.

summarized by Joshua R. Giddings in *The Exiles of Florida*, published in 1858. "Power is never more dangerous than when wielded by military men," he wrote. "They usually feel ambitious to display their own prowess, and that of the troops under their command; and no person can read the communications of General Gaines, in regard to the Exiles who had gathered in and around this fort, without feeling conscious that he greatly desired to give to the people of the United States an example of the science and power by which they could destroy human life."

After the destruction of the fort, Giddings commented on what happened to the black survivors, "They were placed on board the gunboats, and their wounds were dressed by the surgeons; and those who recovered were afterwards delivered over to claimants in Georgia. Those who were slightly wounded, but able to travel, were taken back with Colonel Clinch to Georgia and delivered over to men who claimed to have descended from planters who, some three to four generations previously, owned the ancestors of the prisoners. There could be no proof of identity, nor was there any court authorized to take testimony, or enter decree in such case; but they were delivered over upon *claim*, taken to the interior, and sold to different planters. There they mingled with that mass of chattelized humanity which characterizes our Southern States, and were swallowed up in that tide of oppression which is now bearing three millions of human beings to untimely graves."

A far bloodier war than the First Seminole War would help to answer moral questions posed by the occupation and destruction of Negro Fort.

Fort Gadsden historic site in the Apalachicola National Forest.

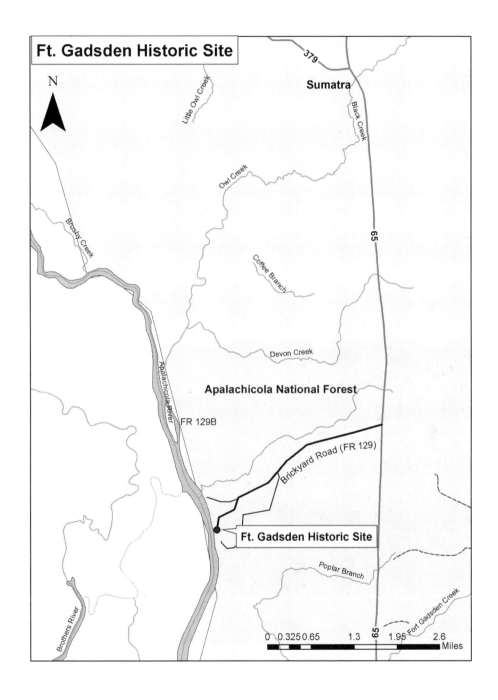

Ft. Gadsden Historic Site

Getting There

Fort Gadsden Historic Site can be accessed from the Gulf Coast by turning north onto State Road 65 just east of Eastpoint and traveling almost 21 miles before turning left onto Forest Road 129 and following the signs. From the north, turn south onto State Road 65 off Highway 20 at Hosford and travel more than 33 miles through the Apalachicola National Forest before turning right onto Forest Road 129. The site is open daily during daylight hours. No camping is allowed, although there are Forest Service campgrounds in the region. Bring bug repellent during warm months.

Nature trail leading to the cemetery at the Fort Gadsden Historic Site.

Four
At the Crossroads

---

*From the Apalachicola River, the Seminole Trail winds east to the confluence of the Wakulla and St. Marks Rivers. Here, a Spanish fort served as a base of operations for Andrew Jackson and a huge army during the First Seminole War as he tried to rid Spanish Florida of the threat posed by Seminoles to the young United States. The fort's ruins can be visited at the **San Marcos de Apalache Historic State Park** in the town of St. Marks, twenty miles south of Tallahassee.*

After the destruction of the Negro Fort, with increased hostilities along the Apalachicola River and in other parts of the region, Florida Creek Indians friendly to the Americans were worried that they would be targeted by the army for simply being Indian. A delegation led by William Perryman visited Fort Scott and spoke with General Gaines. Gaines was forthright in his response: "The President, wishing to do justice to his red friends and children, has given orders for the bad to be separated from the good. Those who have taken up arms against him,

San Marcos de Apalachee Historic State Park entrance.

and such as have listened to the bad talks of the people beyond the sea, must go to Mickasukee or Suwany, where we wish to find them together. But all those who were our friends in the war will sit still at their homes in peace; we will pay them for what corn and meat they have to sell to us; we will be their friends, and when they are hungry we will give them meat. The hostile party pretend to calculate on help from the British! They may as well look for soldiers from the moon to help them."

During the harsh winter of 1817–1818, one made more difficult by the eruption of the Indonesian volcano of Tambora that clouded the atmosphere, Andrew Jackson amassed his troops for a Florida raid. The bulk of the force consisted of more than 2,000 Tennessee and Georgia militia, and Creek chief William McIntosh contributed 1,500 warriors. The motivation for McIntosh was obvious—fight the Seminoles and be allowed to stay in his south Georgia homeland where he had set up an elaborate plantation complete with slaves.

Once the massive force began their march along the Apalachicola River in March of 1818, it was the largest army to have entered Florida since Governor Moore raided the Apalachee more than a century before. Upon reaching the old Negro Fort site and ordering James Gadsden to rebuild it, Jackson marched toward Tallahassee and the community of Miccosukee near the Georgia border in search of Seminoles. Crossing the Ochlockonee River was a task.

"On the 25th we drew what provisions we could carry on our backs and set out toward the Mackasooky town," wrote Private John Banks of the Georgia militia in his journal. "The next Sunday following we came to the Oconochy river. All hands set to building canoes, the river being very high that night, and the next day we crossed the river."

On March 31, Jackson reached the village of Tallahassee Talofa, located in the present-day city limits of Tallahassee. Understandably, the village was abandoned—Jackson's force was simply too large to take on in a pitched battle—but as the force headed east towards Lake Miccosukee, they encountered a Seminole rear guard as Miccosukee villagers fled. At the village site, they found a scalp pole with scalps taken from the Scott party along the Apalachicola River the previous November.

Undeterred, Jackson then marched to the Spanish fort at the confluence of the Wakulla and St. Marks Rivers. San Marcos de Apalache was about twenty miles south of present-day Tallahassee. With his intimidating show of force, Jackson seized the fort without firing a shot. He set up his own civil government, and announced the capture of Florida for the United States.

By ruse, Jackson soon captured the Red Stick Creek Himollemico and the Creek/Seminole chief Josiah Francis, also known as the Prophet Francis. Francis Town, named after Francis, was about three miles upriver along the Wakulla River just below the present-day Highway 98 Bridge. Himollemico and Francis were hanged without trial.

A few days earlier, Duncan McKrimmon—a lost Georgia militia-man in Jackson's force—was captured by Francis' warriors and taken to Francis Town. When McKrimmon was about to be executed in retaliation for the deaths of sisters of one of his captors, the chief's fifteen-year-old daughter, Malee (called "Milly" by the Americans), pleaded for his life. The brother of the killed sisters relented and the young soldier was spared. McKrimmon was taken to Fort San Marcos and ransomed to the Spanish. Afterwards, the story of Milly Francis—"Florida's Pocohontas"—was widely circulated in the United States. Milly was removed to the western Indian Territory with other Creeks and Seminoles. She died in 1848 before she could receive the pension and medal Congress had authorized for her.

The hanging of the Prophet Francis has troubled some Jackson biographers. Historian Clifton Paisley, in his *The Red Hills of Florida, 1528–1865,* explains why: "Francis had most of the virtues that Americans valued—courage, dignity, compassion, and the rest. He was, as one Jackson biographer reported, 'humane in his disposition, by no means barbarous—a model chief.' His manners were pleasing, he conversed well in English and Spanish, and he was a man of comfortable wealth, with property that included a number of slaves. The only thing Jackson had against him was that he was also a Creek patriot, opposing the march of Manifest Destiny—but patriotism was also a virtue. Instead of placing Francis before a firing squad, and thereby giving him a death more honorable, Jackson decreed that he should receive the execution of a villain."

Three weeks later, two captured British nationals—the Scottish trader Alexander Arbuthnot and British marine captain Richard Ambrister—were found guilty of aiding the Indians by a military court at the fort and initially sentenced to death. The court relented to pleas for clemency and changed the sentence to fifty lashes and a year in prison. Jackson would have none of it. He insisted that the original sentence be carried out and on the morning of April 29, Ambrister was shot by firing squad and Arbuthnot was hanged from the yardarm of his own vessel.

Jackson lost few men due to fighting during his Florida raid, although his men found Fort San Marcos de Apalachee inhospitable, even in springtime. Several men died of disease and were buried a short distance away. Their remains were reinterred closer to the fort soon after the state of Florida established a state park at the site in 1964.

Jackson's capture and occupation of San Marcos de Apalache was simply another footnote in the fort's storied history. First built in 1679 by the Spanish as a way to protect their defenseless missionary priests from being kidnapped and held for ransom by pirates, the fort was constructed of logs and coated with lime to create the appearance of stone. It failed to discourage pirates, however, who raided it several times and finally set it afire.

By the turn of the next century, the fort and surrounding area had become a frontier pawn in the intense tug of war between European countries trying to control Florida. The British and their Creek allies destroyed nearby missions in 1704, capturing Apalachees as slaves and driving the remaining Indians to other lands. British raids became more frequent, and in 1739, Spain finally replaced the fort's logs with limestone that was dug from beneath the saw palmetto and cut with axes while still soft. Eventually, the wet limestone became hard as granite. Better able to withstand human invaders, the fort was still no match for natural forces. The forty members of the Spanish garrison were drowned by a hurricane in 1758.

In 1800, a British deserter, William Augustus Bowles, who had married a Creek woman, led four hundred Seminole and Creek Indians to capture the fort. He sought to create an Indian nation and set himself up as "King of Florida." He held the fort for five weeks until Spain reclaimed it and occupied it until Jackson's enormous force arrived.

After leaving San Marcos de Apalache in the spring of 1818, Jackson drove his troops east to the Suwannee River where he had a running battle with Seminoles led by Peter McQueen, and later along the Suwannee River at Bowlegs Town. Again, Jackson's forces were too large for a pitched battle, so the Seminoles mostly employed rear guard actions to allow women and children to escape, something with which the Seminoles would grow accustomed during the latter part of the Second Seminole War. Jackson then traveled west to capture Spanish Pensacola, making his foray into Florida complete.

Jackson's actions appalled many in his own government and incurred the wrath of both Spain and Great Britain, but it made Spain realize the difficulty in maintaining control of Florida. Three years later, in 1821, partly to stem the controversy, the United States purchased Florida. It marked the end of Florida's centuries-long Spanish era.

If you walk the stone ruins of San Marcos de Apalache today, the scent of honeysuckle will likely permeate the air in spring. Birds will sing sweetly and the sounds of boats and fishermen drift from the nearby Wakulla and St. Marks Rivers. The long abandonment of the fort has allowed live oak, sabal palm, and red cedar to grow to impressive sizes. Spanish moss sways in the breeze. And the early Spanish moats are now filled with purple flag irises and other wetland plants.

Nothing about the ruins reveals the strategic importance of the spot, how for almost two centuries, Native Americans, Spanish, British, Americans, pirates, and Confederates wrestled for control of the fort and the region.

The area of San Marcos de Apalache remains a strategic spot today, but more for recreation. It is the terminus for bicyclists on the 16-mile Tallahassee–St. Marks Historic Railroad State Trail, and it's also the confluence of two scenic rivers—the St. Marks and Wakulla—a spot frequented by paddlers and boaters.

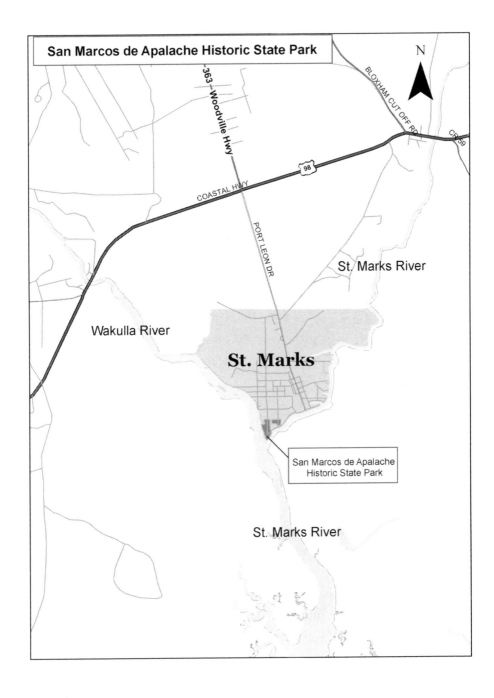

Part of the early Spanish wall at San Marcos de Apalachee Historic State Park.

Getting There

You can visit the San Marcos de Apalache Historic State Park from 9 a.m. to 5 p.m. Thursday through Monday by driving south of Tallahassee about twenty miles on Highway 353 to the town of St. Marks. When you reach the St. Marks River at the stop sign, turn right onto Old Fort Road and travel about another mile until you reach the fort site. You can tour the historic fort site free of charge, although there is a small admission charge for the museum. There are several restaurants in St. Marks along with a bed and breakfast. The address is 148 Old Fort Road, St. Marks, FL 32355; (850) 925-6216.

Other historic sites from the First Seminole War include the town of Old Town near the Suwannee River along Highway 19/98. This was where Jackson's forces destroyed Bowlegs Town. A sign along the main highway describes the history.

Jackson's route through north Florida is commonly known as The Jackson Trail. The trail generally ran alongside present-day Highway 19, but it branched to the south towards the coast. Along present-day Horseshoe Beach Road (Highway 351) about 16 miles south of Cross City along the east side of the road, it is believed that Jackson and his army camped at a freshwater pond. The spot is now a park and known as the Jackson Watering Hole. A historic marker describes the Jackson Trail.

Five
War's Beginning

After the First Seminole War, most Seminoles were eventually pressured to occupy a reservation in central Florida, but peace did not last. Andrew Jackson became president of the United States and successfully urged Congress to pass the Indian Removal Act, which authorized the removal of Southeastern tribes—including the Seminoles—to "Indian Territory" west of the Mississippi River. Tensions mounted and fighting eventually broke out in 1835.

*The Seminole Trail now leads us to central Florida near present-day Bushnell to the **Dade Historic Battlefield State Park**, where the first large battle of the Second Seminole War was fought—a decisive victory for the Seminoles.*

"This is a negro not an Indian war." — General Thomas Sidney Jesup, December 9, 1836

A common first impression of the Dade Historic Battlefield State Park near Bushnell is that it is beautiful. Arching old-growth live oaks adorned with swaying strands of Spanish moss canopy the site. And the visitors center is bordered by an aged cedar tree—sacred to the Seminoles—and lush coontie palms. The roots of the coontie, a Seminole word meaning "flour root," were extensively used by the natives as flour, but only after the plant's poison was carefully leached out.

While the visitors center shows the history of the Seminoles and the battle in large panels and a diorama, a short trail around the battlefield site provides a more complete picture. The site is marked by three white pillars where Major Francis Dade and two of his officers fell. The marshy area that was at the soldiers' backside during the battle is still visible just across a fence on private land to the east, and a small triangular breastwork has been erected by the park service to give an idea of the soldiers' defensive position. No living person today can describe the battle that ignited the seven-year Second Seminole War. Only historic accounts from a handful of survivors and the Seminole leader Alligator—along with an annual reenactment—bring it to life.

Three days after Christmas, December 28, 1835, Major Dade was leading 107 men from Fort Brooke near Tampa to Fort King near Ocala on the twenty-foot wide, one-hundred-mile path known as the Fort King Road. A large group of Seminoles and black allies—by some estimates about 180 warriors—had followed the column for several days and found an ideal spot to lay in wait for an ambush. They were led by Micanopy, Jumper (Ote Emathla), and Alligator. Osceola, who would later become a famous Seminole war leader, had other plans. He was lying in wait at Fort King in order to kill Indian agent Wiley Thompson. Thompson had enraged Osceola when he captured his black wife and sent her into slavery. Osceola had been arrested in the fracas and briefly put in chains, and now Osceola was bent on revenge.

The reasons for the Seminoles' hostility were clear—they were being pressured to leave Florida and move to unfamiliar western lands, and many Black Seminoles would be forced back into slavery. Osceola's attack on Thompson, and Micanopy and Jumper's attack on Dade, would be their defiant statement. They would fight to stay in their homeland.

The first deadly Seminole volley of the battle was at Dade's advance guard, and this initial blow struck down Major Dade and two of his officers. Dade was the first to be hit, shot through the heart by Micanopy's own gun. Louis Pacheco, a black interpreter and guide for the soldiers and survivor of the battle, described the scene right after Dade was shot: "I ... saw the Indians rise up like a string of pepper in a streak of light. They had on only breachclouts and moccasins. Their bodies were painted red, and when they fired it looked as though lightning flashed along the whole length of the line. Every man of the advance guard fell. Consternation filled the troops. You could see them waver and tremble. Then the voice of a command rang out and they remained firm. I thought I had seen the last day of the world. I... laid down behind a pine tree, beating my head against it and praying." Pacheco was spared by the advancing Seminoles only because he was a Negro and claimed to be a slave. Being educated, he would later help the Seminoles as an interpreter and in reading captured documents.

Ransom Clark, another survivor, also described the deadly attack after Dade fell: "...a volley as if from a thousand rifles was poured in upon us from the front, and all along our left flank. I looked around me, and it seemed as if I was the only one left standing in the right wing. Neither could I, until several other vollies had been fired at us, see an enemy, —and when I did, I could only see their heads and arms peering out from the long grass far and near, and from behind the pine trees."

About half of Dade's command had fallen in the first few minutes of deadly firing, with Seminoles seeming to be shooting from behind every tree and clump of palmetto. With the advance guard extinguished, Captain George Gardiner took command. He defiantly drew a sword, cursed, and bellowed orders. "Bring up the gun!" he cried. He knew that the six-pound cannon, shooting canister and grape shot, would disperse the attackers better than musket balls, and it would serve as a rallying point for the men.

Alligator, known by the Seminoles as Halpatter Tustenugee (Alligator Warrior), later recalled the sight of Gardiner boldly standing amidst the melee: "a little man, a great brave, who shook his sword at the soldiers and said, 'God damn!' No rifle ball could hit him."

With a small marshy pond at their back and a semicircle of attacking Seminoles before them, the remaining soldiers ducked behind trees

Man portraying Captain George Gardiner at the 2011 Dade Battle Reenactment.

and returned fire. Most of the Seminole warriors were also concealed behind trees and thick palmettos, so defensive efforts by the soldiers were largely ineffective. When the cannon was pointed in their direction, warriors ducked and laid flat as cannonballs hurled through the piney woods, splintering branches and trees. They resumed firing once the smoke cleared. And as for the soldiers handling the cannon, they were fully exposed in doing their duties and were quickly cut down, while Lieutenant William Basinger of the artillery unit ordered other men to take their places. Eventually, the cannon fire was effective in pushing back the Seminoles. A brief lull allowed the surviving men to build a triangular breastwork from the pines for protection and for Dr. John Slade Gatlin to begin treating the wounded. The living also began stripping the dead of ammunition, knowing it would be needed. Only about forty able-bodied men remained.

Alligator rallied the warriors for another attack, with some Seminoles advancing on horseback. "The woods rang with warwhoops," wrote Ransom Clark, "and the crack of their rifles was as one incessant peal of sharp ringing bells, to which the loud reports of musketry and the booming of the artillery formed a fitting though fearful accompaniment."

Inside the log enclosure, men fell from volleys of gunfire. Clark, nearly crippled from five gunshots, observed how the cannon was finally silenced; the portfire match had gone out. In all, he said it had been fired 49 times. Captain Gardiner, blood running from a half dozen wounds, spoke his last. "I can give you no more orders. my lads. Do your best!"

Doctor Gatlin braced himself with two double-barreled shotguns. "Well, I have got four barrels for them!" he cried.

The end came about six hours after the first shot was fired. The shooting ceased. No soldiers could offer resistance. The mass of Seminoles approached the enclosure. Clark played dead, not a difficult task given his wounds, although two other soldiers jumped up and fought

Man portraying Dr. Gatlin at the 2011 Dade Battle Reenactment.

briefly before being struck down. The Seminoles stripped the dead of guns and what little ammunition that remained, but did not take jewelry, money, or other items. A group of escaped slaves, not part of the actual battle, later mutilated some of the bodies. The lone cannon was pried off its carriage with broken muskets and bayonets and heaved into the nearby pond.

Three white soldiers survived the massacre, but one was later killed by a Seminole on horseback as he helped Ransom Clark return to Fort Brooke, sixty miles to the south. The fact that Clark crawled and staggered most of the distance alone in three days was a miracle, a testament to human will and stamina. The night before he reached the fort, Clark was "a good deal annoyed by the wolves who had scented my blood, and came very close to me."

On New Year's Day, a second survivor, Joseph Sprague, made it to the fort with an arm wound. He confirmed Clark's account of the battle while cries of mourning and calls for revenge filled the region. The Seminoles, on the other hand, celebrated their victory in the nearly impenetrable Cove of the Withlacoochee to the north, a junglelike area of swamps, forests, and hammocks bordered on nearly three sides by the curving Withlacoochee River. In Alligator's account of the battle, written down by a guard after Alligator's capture in 1838, he claimed that only three warriors were killed and five wounded.

Eight weeks after the Dade battle, an Army contingent of about a thousand men marched north from Fort Brooke on the Fort King Road. Each night, they erected a log breastwork three feet high, posted pickets, and the men slept with their guns, fearing attack. After eight days, they spotted a multitude of buzzards, and they knew they had reached the battlefield site. Twenty-three-year-old Second Lieutenant James Duncan described the haunting scene: "The first indication of our proximity were the soldiers' shoes and clothing, soon after a skeleton then another! then another! Soon we came upon the scene in all its horrors. Gracious God what a sight. The vultures rose in clouds as the approach of the column drove them from their prey, the very breastwork was black with them. Some hovered over us as we looked upon the scene before us whilst others settled upon the adjoining trees waiting for our departure, in order to return to their prey."

The breastwork that Dade's soldiers had erected was riddled with bullet holes, and so were outlying trees that had sheltered Seminole warriors. Also, trees in various directions had been cut down by cannonballs.

Next came the gruesome process of identifying the bodies, some by insignia and others by personal items in their pockets and traits such as gold teeth. Most of the skeletal bodies lay where they had fallen, and so it was easy to mark the spot where the officers had succumbed to Seminole bullets. Today, those locations are marked by tall white pillars at the battlefield site.

The Dade Massacre, as it was often called during the war, sent shockwaves through the young country of the United States. On January 5, only days after the battle, Major Francis Belton wrote: "The best in the army lie bleaching in the air, defaced by Negroes and torn [by] obscene birds—Rouse up Florida." The battle became a rallying cry for armed forces recruitment, and thousands heeded the call. The battle was only the beginning of a long and drawn-out seven-year war, one in which Florida's hostile terrain and climate were as much an enemy to the soldiers as was the stealth of the Seminoles. It was a battle that the Seminoles clearly won but one that eventually marked the near end of their world, much like the elimination of George Armstrong Custer and the Seventh Calvary by Plains Indians decades later.

Reenactment

Moses Jumper Jr. bore the countenance of a man who had just won a battle, and in some ways he had. The 2011 Dade Battlefield Reenactment had just concluded on the 175th anniversary of the battle, and Jumper—whose great-great-great-uncle was the famous Seminole war leader Jumper who fought in the battle—was on the prevailing side. "This was a great Seminole victory," he said, sitting atop a brown horse that was descended from early Spanish horses brought to Florida centuries before. "For us to surprise and wipe out that many soldiers, we had to have everything on the ball, everything going for us. This is a good reenactment. I hope the public grasps the reality of how the war was actually fought."

Jumper and other family members from the Big Cypress Seminole Reservation have been involved with the reenactment for a decade "with the blessings of the Seminole tribe." When asked how it felt to partici-

Members of the Seminole Tribe of Florida at the 2011 Dade Battle Reenactment
from left to right: Chebon Gooden, Andre Jumper, Moses Jumper Jr., and Blevyns
Jumper (foreground).

Soldiers under fire building breastworks at the 2011 Dade Battle Reenactment.

pate in the mock battle, only two hundred yards from where the actual shots were fired, Jumper's voice quieted and he leaned over. "I feel like I'm one of my ancestors. I'm actually part of the battle."

During the reenactment, a large crowd of onlookers filled bleachers or sat on grass behind a rope barrier. A small cleared area lay before them against a backdrop of thick piney woods and an understory of tall grass and palmetto. A man dressed in a period soldier's uniform stepped before the crowd and, in a pained voice, began narrating the battle— "This is where it happened; this is where they fell." In real life, his name was Kent Lowe, but on this day, he portrayed Ransom Clark, one of only three surviving soldiers. (For years Ransom Clark was played by Frank Laumer, who wrote a riveting fictional account of Clark and the battle in a book called *Nobody's Hero.*)

Soon, a man portraying Major Francis Dade, a striking figure in blue uniform on horseback, led a group of foot soldiers dressed in woolen uniforms and wearing the tall dark hats of the day. "We have now got through all danger," he shouted. "Keep up good heart, and when we get to Fort King, I'll give you three days off for Christmas!" The soldiers cheered. The original company, its purpose being to reinforce Fort King, had been marching for six days under constant threat of Seminole attack, and they were just starting to relax. Since the weather on that fateful day was cold and rainy, many carried their muskets and cartridge boxes under their overcoats.

As the column slowly approached the main clearing and began to enter the piney woods, onlookers familiar with the battle knew what would happen next. Shots suddenly rang out from Seminoles in concealed positions, and Major Dade cried "My God!" before he fell. A frenzy of confusion followed as soldiers tried to find cover and return fire, while others staggered and clutched wounds. Seminoles popped up from various positions and fired. Soldiers fell as they scrambled to load and fire their six-pound cannon. Loud booms soon echoed through the forest as white smoke clouds hovered like ghosts.

Reenactors effectively portrayed key figures in the battle. There was Captain George Gardiner, cursing and waving a sword—"God damn!" he frequently cried, true to accounts. Lieutenant Basinger kept the troops focused on manning the cannon, while Dr. Gatlin tried to tend the wounded, his face noticeably strained. And at the end, when the Seminoles stealthily moved in among the fallen bodies of their quarry, a man portraying Private Joseph Wilson—a musician—jumped up, grabbed a warrior's rifle and clubbed him before attempting to flee. He was promptly shot down. The battle was over. After the Seminoles left, another man portraying Ransom Clark was seen being assisted by fellow survivor Edwin DeCourcy. True to the story, however, DeCourcy was later cut down by a Seminole on horseback while Clark lay concealed. Clark was left to make the long agonizing journey back to Fort Brooke by himself.

The guns quiet, a bugler played the haunting "Taps" to a hushed crowd, and just for a moment, it seemed that the battle was real and the men who had fallen would not rise again. But after a couple of minutes, they did begin to move and stand up—slowly—as if waking from a dream. They lined up in formation before the audience. Seminoles emerged from the woods and faced the crowd as well, and both groups cleared their weapons to loud applause. The rope barrier was dropped, and members of the public freely mingled with the reenactors.

John Griffin, a Black Seminole elder from Groveland with long gray hair that resembled Spanish moss, clutched a recently used musket. "I feel like we're incarnating the spirit of that time," he said. Several family members had joined him, descendents of a slave who escaped an Alabama plantation and joined the Seminoles during the Second Seminole War near present-day Brooksville at a village known as Chocachattee (Red House).

Black Seminole John Griffin at the 2011 Dade Battle Reenactment.

Black Seminole Mathew Griffin at the
2011 Dade Battle Reenactment.

Matthew Griffin, 19, grand-nephew of the elder Griffin, had been participating since he was ten years old. "I feel like we're honoring our ancestors by telling our story," he said. Griffin, a college student majoring in agricultural business at Florida A&M University, joins family members for several reenactments each year. The events help to bind them together, he said, and he has befriended several other reenactors, such as the Seminoles from Big Cypress. Many are on a type of Seminole war circuit. There is the Dade Reenactment during the first weekend in January, the Battle of Okeechobee Reenactment in early February, the Fort Foster Rendezvous in mid-February, the Big Cypress Shootout in late February on the Big Cypress Seminole Reservation, and Fort Cooper Days near Inverness in mid-March. New festivals and reenactments are in the works.

Not all Seminole reenactors have Seminole ancestry. A gray-haired man in Seminole garb and wearing a turban, his face fully painted in black and brown, only described himself as *Penwv*, Muscogee for "turkey." At first he stayed in character when speaking: "They're not sending me to Arkansas. It's too cold there and the wind blows all the time. I'm an old man and I'm not going. I come from the *Pah-hay-o-kee*, the River of Grass, and I will not go north of the Okefenokee." Getting out of character just for a moment, *Penwv* said with a smile, "I'm a fourth-generation cracker." "Cracker" is a term used for Florida's early white pioneers and cattle drovers.

Unity between races and honoring American men and women in uniform were also themes for the event. A park service official noted that reenactors from both sides had once served in the American armed services, "so now these people are on the same side."

Perhaps the reenactment's purpose was best put in perspective in a short essay produced by the Dade Battlefield Society: "The war would last seven years, claim thousands of lives, cost thirty million dollars and force the removal of virtually all Seminoles to Oklahoma. With peace, all of Florida was open to white settlement. The fields that had been battlegrounds have become a nation's playground. Money, lives and honor paid for this land. Perhaps now it is our responsibility to plant instead of cut, to protect instead of kill, to see that the rivers again run clean. We cannot undo the past, but we can study it, learn from it, and in so doing honor the sacrifices of all races."

Begun in 1980, the Dade battle reenactment occurs during the first weekend of January, both Saturday and Sunday. Saturday is usually the

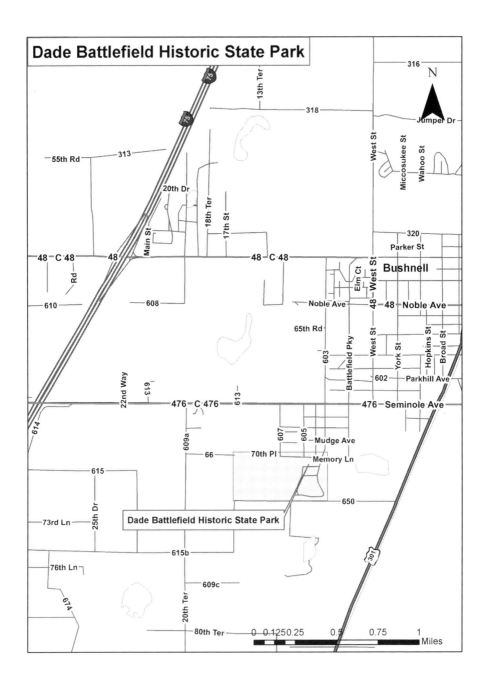

Dade Battlefield Historic State Park

busier day, depending on weather. Visitors are encouraged to come early to get a good viewing spot. Living history reenactors portray Seminoles, soldiers, traders, and settlers of the period. While the shooting begins around 2 p.m. both Saturday and Sunday, other offerings include period camps of the different parties, tomahawk throwing and musket shooting contests, a trade fair, historic arts and crafts demonstrations, full-scale cannon firing, tree cutting and barricade building, folk music, and historical lectures.

Getting There

Dade Historic Battlefield State Park is located off I-75 at the Bushnell exit on State Road 48. Travel one mile east of I-75 and look for the signs that point the way on your right. While the park is open from 8 a.m. to sunset 365 days a year, the Visitors Center is open from 9 a.m. to 5 p.m. Thursday through Monday. Check the park website for reenactment and event details or call the headquarters at (352)793-4781. The park also includes a playground, covered picnic shelters, and a recreation hall. No overnight stays are allowed. The address is 7200 County Road 603, Bushnell, Florida, 33513.

Six
Protecting the Bridge

Fort Foster

From the Dade Battlefield, the trail leads to the site of **Fort Foster in Hillsborough River State Park** *northeast of Tampa. Here, American soldiers sought to protect a vital bridge over the Hillsborough River along the Fort King Military Road to keep supplies moving between forts and to efficiently move armies intent on destroying or capturing the Seminoles.*

"Florida is certainly the poorest country that ever two people quarreled for. The climate in the first place is objectionable; for even in winter, while persons further north were freezing, we were melting with heat. ... It is in fact a most hideous region to live in; a perfect paradise for Indians, alligators, serpents, frogs, and every other kind of loathsome reptile."—Jacob Rhett Motte, 1838, *Journey into Wilderness*

The bridge over the Hillsborough River at Fort Foster.

To better understand what American soldiers endured during the Second Seminole War, put on a thick wool jacket and trousers, hoist a heavy musket and backpack, and walk a ways down the remnant stretch of the Fort King Military Road in Hillsborough River State Park near Tampa. Make sure it's during the heat of the day and at a time of year when any rest in the shade will invite swarms of mosquitoes and maybe a yellow fly or ten. It will soon become apparent why the majority of soldiers died from malaria and other sicknesses during the war rather than from Seminole bullets.

Another factor that becomes apparent in Florida's challenging climate is that the heat and bugs often help to dull the senses, making one more vulnerable to ambushes. This often occurred along the hundred-mile military road, and not just in regards to Major Dade's detachment. The Seminoles were extremely skilled at hit-and-run attacks, shooting from one position, popping up in another, and then vanishing before an effective counterattack could be launched.

The Hillsborough River was a major obstacle along the military road. It might take two days to ferry a supply train across the river, and soldiers were vulnerable to attack once in the low trough of the river. A bridge was the optimal solution. But bridges were only made from wood during that time period and Seminoles frequently burned wood bridges. Therefore, a fort was built at the bridge site for the sole purpose of protecting the bridge. Originally, it was known as Fort Alabama, named after the Alabama volunteers who initially built the fort and occupied it for only two months. Their occupation was a lively one, however, since major Seminole attacks occurred on two occasions.

Regarding one attack, a veteran soldier noted, "…being unable, however, to make any impression upon the garrison, by which they [Seminoles] were warmly and cordially received, a number of them ascended the trees which overlooked the pickets, and thence wounded several men. One of them being observed by a Rifleman, was fired at and hit: the wound given being so severe, that the blood was seen to trickle down the tree. Notwithstanding the extent of this injury, the savage succeeded in descending, and made off with himself and rifle. From this incident, the difficulty of catching an Indian alive may be inferred."

When a large detachment of enlisted men escorted the Alabama Volunteers from the fort in late April, soon after the onset of mosquito season, they left a loaded musket aimed into a keg of black powder inside the fort's magazine. If the door was opened, a string tied to the trigger would fire the musket. Soon after the soldiers left the fort, they heard a tremendous explosion and it was later determined that two curious Seminoles had been killed by the booby trap. The column fell under attack on their way to Fort Brooke and this was known as the Battle of

Clonoto Lassa (Thonotosassa Lake).

The abandoned Fort Alabama and bridge were burned by the Seminoles only to be reconstructed again in late 1836. It was called Fort Foster after the man who directed its construction, Lieutenant-Colonel William S. Foster. Besides protecting the bridge, the sturdier new fort would serve as a supply depot.

A six-pound cannon was aimed at the bridge site at all times. Trees were cleared around the fort and bridge site for a hundred yards or more, and troops were stationed around the fort and on both sides of the bridge. Bonfires outside the fort were kept burning all night in order to detect stealthy Seminoles.

Today, in Hillsborough River State Park, visitors can tour Fort Foster, one of only two completely reconstructed Second Seminole War–era forts out of more than two hundred that were originally built. The other reconstructed fort is Fort Christmas twenty miles east of Orlando. In

The reconstructed Fort Foster in Hillsborough River State Park.

addition, the old barracks of Fort Dallas in Miami's Lummus Park still stands as a reminder of the era. See chapter eleven for details about these other sites.

Visitors to Fort Foster gather at the park's modest interpretive center at designated times—2 p.m. on Saturdays; 11 a.m. on Sundays (weather permitting)—for a tour of the fort. After paying a small fee, they climb into a van and are ferried across Highway 301 to a dirt parking lot. Then they walk through a heavily wooded area down the old military road. During most months on the third weekend (hot summer months are sometimes skipped) a surprise awaits modern travelers. War cries shatter the stillness of the piney woods. Muskets pop and armed and painted Seminoles pop out from behind palmetto bushes and advance toward the line of visitors. Soldiers race out from the fort to defend the visitors and escort them to safety inside the log walls. It's a more realis-

Inside the general store at the reconstructed Fort Foster.

tic type of haunted trail and it doesn't take much imagination to elicit a rush of adrenalin.

Once inside the fort, tour guides provide a fairly grim picture of life on the Florida frontier. Only officers and the sick and injured stayed inside the fort's cabins, but without air conditioning or even a fan, it could be sweltering. And smudge pots smoldered in every building to ward off mosquitoes. Still, one didn't have to worry about being picked off by a Seminole sniper, unlike the enlisted men and volunteers staying in tents outside the walls.

The fort's commissary has been outfitted with the tools and implements of the day. Several wood barrels are stacked inside since this is how food was stored. For transport, the heavy barrels could be rolled instead of carried.

The infirmary was clearly a place where soldiers didn't want to end up. There was no anesthesia in those days, and leeches were heavily used. If in doubt about an injured limb, amputation was commonplace. The infirmary had three tiers of bunk beds. If you were on the lower bunk, that meant you had a good chance of survival. The middle bunk? Maybe a 50-50 chance. The top bunk meant you were doomed and just waiting out your limited time on earth.

John Bemrose, stationed in a Fort Drane Army hospital during the Second Seminole War, provides a grim description of a frontier infirmary like that found at Fort Foster: "When I went along those sheds of a morning to administer to each man his remedy," he writes in *Reminisces of the Second Seminole War,* "I really felt disgraced and humbled to see fine athletic fellows in the lowest state of misery and thoroughly cast down by the magnitude of their discomforts.

"One would exclaim, 'Steward, for mercy's sake get me out of this!' Another would groan deplorably, saying, 'I shall be steamed before the day is over.' Sand flies and mosquitoes were innumerable, all adding to their troubles. Centipedes, cockroaches, scorpions, with immense spi-

Three tiers of beds in the Fort Foster infirmary. If a wounded man was assigned to the top bunk, it meant that he had little hope of survival.

ders, were daily tenants of the place, and at night we were surrounded by myriads of wolves who kept up a continual yelling. This, with the croaking of immense bullfrogs, was not conducive to rest. The sand of the fort was full of chigoes [chiggers], and a sort of black flea. This latter was the greatest [pest] to all of us."

Even when it is not the third weekend of the month, when Seminoles raid the oncoming group of visitors, reenactors often greet visitors at the fort. Sometimes, a man dressed as a Creek Indian scout, complete with traditional long coat, tomahawk pipe and musket, addresses the people with a proper Muscogee greeting—*Hangschee, Stong-go* (hello, how are you?). He highlights the reasons why these close relatives of the Seminoles helped the Army. "We don't want to be sent to the western lands," he begins. "The best way to do this is to volunteer and fight with the soldiers against the renegades. These people [Seminoles] are our relatives. We know their ways because they come from our people. But they are renegades.

"Even though we serve as scouts and warriors for the Army, and we hunt game to increase their food supply, we are treated differently. We are treated as savages." The McIntosh Creeks, or "white sticks" as they sometimes called themselves, had adopted many European ways and some even had plantations and slaves. But despite their service to the Army and attempts at adaptation, most met with the same fate as the Seminoles—they were ultimately moved west.

After Colonel Foster supervised the fort's construction, he moved on to build a similar fort and bridge along the Withlacoochee River near present-day Dade City. Foster left behind a contingent of seventy men and volunteers to garrison the fort, named Fort Dade for the major killed in the battle that started the Second Seminole War (see Chapter Five). It wasn't long before trouble began. Besides picking off soldiers around the fort in their guerilla style of warfare, Seminoles attacked the fort on February 2, 1837, and attempted to burn down the bridge. More attacks followed. Disrupting the supply line from Fort Brooke to Fort King was vital in order for the Seminoles to remain in their stronghold in the Cove of the Withlacoochee.

Seminole attacks let up after a hundred marine reinforcements arrived from Fort Brooke in late February 1837. By April of that year, cases of malaria, typhoid, and dysentery were wreaking havoc on the fort's crowded occupants. "Whenever it rains, the pickets are overflowed and the tents of the soldiers are flooded with water," wrote post physician Dr. J.H. Baldwin. "When this is succeeded by a hot sun, new cases of dysentery and diarrhea invariably occur—some of which are very violent."

Fearing an epidemic, the Army abandoned the fort for the summer and reoccupied it in October. By this time, the Seminoles were being driven farther south into the swamp-laden Florida peninsula, and life at Fort Foster became safer and easier as the garrison was reduced to a few men. They mostly served as the fort's caretakers, ensuring that vengeful Seminoles wouldn't burn the fort. Once hostilities ended, the fort was abandoned and the Florida elements soon erased most obvious signs of its existence. In the early 1960s, a father and son team collected numerous artifacts from the river in front of the fort site, and these are on display at the Frostproof Historical Museum in Frostproof, Florida. The state of Florida followed with archaeological surveys in 1974 soon after two hundred acres of the historic site was donated to the state by the Thomas family. Many of those artifacts are housed in the state park's small museum.

The park service began rebuilding Fort Foster and the bridge on the original site in 1979. "The original basic structure of the fort took a week and a half to build in 1837," said one park ranger. "It took us a year and a half." The fort's original builders were able to use trees on site, while the modern builders had to obtain permits and truck in pressure-treated logs.

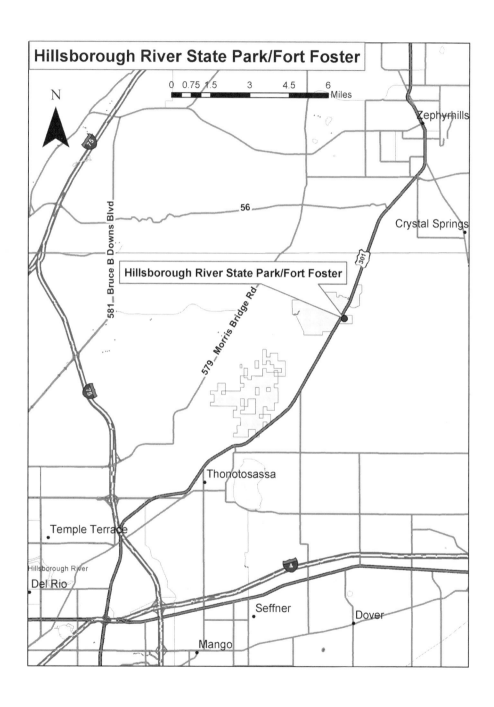

Getting There

H illsborough River State Park is located on U.S. 301 North near Tho-notosassa about 10 miles northeast of Tampa. From I-75, it is easily accessed by taking the Highway 582 (E. Fowler Avenue) exit and trav-eling 1.5 miles east to U.S. 301 and turning left. The park entrance is about 4.5 miles on the left. The park is open 365 days a year from 8 a.m. to sunset, and it features camping, canoe and bike rentals, picnicking, a swimming pool, and more than seven miles of nature trails.

Check the park website for information about the Fort Foster Ren-dezvous, held annually in February: http://www.floridastateparks.org/ fortfoster/default.cfm. Call the park to double-check about weekend tour times through the fort, (813) 987-6771. The fort can only be ac-cessed through a park tour. The address for the state park is 15402 U.S. 301 North, Thonotosassa, FL 33592.

The Frostproof Historical Museum, which houses many historical items from Fort Foster, is located in Frostproof south of I-4 and Lake Wales. It is open from 1 p.m. to 4 p.m. on Saturdays from June through September; and Tuesdays, Thursdays, and Saturdays from October through May. The address is 210 S. Scenic Highway, Frostproof, 33843.

Seven
Sugar Mill Blues

Bulow Ruins

While fighting during the Second Seminole War was raging above Tampa along the military road and in the Cove of the Withlacoochee, Seminole leaders King Philip and his son, Coacoochee (Wildcat), were raiding plantations and associated sugar mills along Florida's northeast coast. So now the Seminole Trail moves to the **Bulow Plantation Ruins Historic State Park** *in the St. Augustine region.*

The Bulow sugar mill ruins forty miles south of St. Augustine resemble the crumbling remnants of an ancient castle. Moss-covered chimneys and ragged remnants of coquina stone walls and arches stand in an artistic array, left to nature's aging processes. Seminoles burned the mill and nearby plantation house in December 1835, the first month of large-scale hostilities during the Second Seminole War, and they were never rebuilt. Not surprisingly, the Bulow ruins and those of other nearby plantations were thought by many in the 1920s and 30s to be the remains of Spanish colonial missions due to the excellent coquina work and archways.

Seminole leaders Coacoochee and his father, King Philip, were familiar with the prosperous Bulow Ville, or Bulowville, before the war broke out. They had supplied its occupants and workers with wild game, honey, and arrowroot in exchange for blankets, calico, gunpowder, and lead, but the war made the friendly relationship take a different turn. The Seminoles became motivated to kill or chase settlers away from the region, and they were largely successful in ending the plantation era of East Florida. At least sixteen large-scale plantations were destroyed and never rebuilt.

Jacob Rhett Motte, a surgeon during the Second Seminole War, described approaching "Bulowville," the common name of Bulow's plantation, soon after it was destroyed. "We turned down the broad avenue, once flanked by noble oaks, but whose scathed and blackened trunks and leafless limbs alone remained to test their former magnificence. On either side were extensive fields, most luxuriant once with richest [sugar] crops, but now presenting a scene o'er which the demon of desolation stalked with unchecked sway. On our left arose through the calm twilight of a summer's evening the ruined arches and columns of the once stately [sugar] Mill; while before us lay a smouldering ashy heap, the only vestige to show where once had stood the hospitable mansion, before the dark demon of ruin commenced his riots."

Later, Motte colorfully described camping at the destroyed mansion: "In the midst of our bivouac stood the remains of Mr. Bulow's mansion, which had been burnt by the Indians; and the scene presented at night was wild and savage in the extreme. Around the fires built amid the ruins, shedding a bright glare in cheerful contrast upon the smoked

Bulow Sugar Mill ruins along Florida's East coast in Bulow Plantation Ruins Historic State Park.

walls, might be seen many recumbent and wrapped up figures; some slumbering, while others listlessly sat watching the glowing embers, resembling brigands in their secret haunts; here and there were displaying haversacks and canteens suspended, and carbines resting against the walls, or the trunk of a tree; while in the back ground, indistinctly visible through the gloom and shadow, were horses picketed, and near them a cloaked sentinel. The moan of the melancholy wind, among the forest trees, with the alternate roar and whistling of the midnight storm, added to the wild and desolate aspect of the scene."

As a byproduct of the Seminoles destroying the East Coast plantations, hundreds of slaves—including 159 from the Bulow Plantation— were enjoined to the Seminole cause, not necessarily by choice. Many found life on the run with the Seminoles no better than slavery, and some escaped and returned to the Americans or found their way to other lands.

Jacob Motte described the arrival of five slaves who escaped the Seminoles and surrendered to the Americans. "They presented a very pitiable spectacle, looking haggard and emaciated, and with no other covering than a cloth about the loins. They complained of having encountered intolerable hardships and very scant fare among the Indians, who gave them nothing to eat but *coonte* and alligators; and that they were subjected to severe beatings on every occurrence of ill temper in their tawny and savage masters. They exhibited the greatest delight at rejoining the whites; and communicated important information relative to the plans and situations of the enemy, whom they represented as reduced to very 'short commons.'"

The Bulow sugar mill had been highly dependent upon slave labor. It was founded by the Prussian Charles W. Bulow, who purchased the 4,675-acre plantation site in 1821. He began to build one of the largest sugar plantations in the United States, but he died only two years later and the plantation fell to his young son, John Bulow. In all, 2,200 acres were cleared for crops using slave labor. Sugar cane was planted on a thousand acres, while other plantation crops included cotton, rice, and indigo. To process the cane, John Bulow built an enormous sugar mill powered by steam energy. In a good year, the mill produced 1.2 million pounds of sugar, or 1,200 pounds per acre. By comparison, a modern sugar operation produces about 1,600 pounds per acre, so the Bulow Plantation was productive for its time, but slaves worked around the clock during the fall sugar-making season. When the sugar mill was not operating, the steam boiler was used to power the plantation sawmill.

By some accounts, John Bulow was a delightful host to several high-profile guests, among them the noted ornithologist and painter John James Audubon. "During the whole long stay with Mr. Bulow," Audubon wrote, "there was no abatement of his kindness, or his unremitted efforts to make me comfortable, and to promote my researches, I shall ever feel grateful to one of the most deserving and generous of men." Bulow often took Audubon on expeditions by sailboat whereupon the painter could shoot birds to paint as subjects.

By other accounts, John Bulow's reputation was wanting. "He had three hundred hands, and although possessed of great wealth was despised by his brother planters because of his cruelty," wrote John Bemrose in *Reminiscences of the Second Seminole War.* "When I saw him, he was quite young and handsome, yet I never heard of a good trait in his character. Dissipated, and quarrelsome with his equals, tyrannical to his dependents, his hands dyed red with the blood of three of his slaves! Truly earth groaned under him and Hell must have groaned for him! The third slave he murdered while I was in the city. The poor negro was attending as marker, during one of his shooting matches, and he happened to make some mistake or blunder. This raised the master's anger and he immediately shot him dead."

And so for a slave, the choices were dreary: live with the Seminoles on the run with scant food resources, or suffer abuse as a slave. Along the nature trail leading to the Bulow sugar mill ruins, the only visible remnants of 46 slave cabins are two foundation stones protruding from the forest floor.

Regarding Bulow's views of the Seminoles, he disagreed with Andrew Jackson's edict to send Seminoles to western lands. Once hostilities broke out, he even resisted occupation by Major Benjamin Putnam and his troops by firing a four-pound cannon at the approaching force. Bulow lost the skirmish and Putnam occupied the plantation and held Bulow as prisoner. After several unsuccessful skirmishes with the Seminoles, however, the plantation was abandoned and settlers in the entire region were ordered to evacuate to St. Augustine. Thus, the abandoned mansions and sugar mills were left to Seminole torches.

Whether the Indians knew of Bulow's feelings regarding the war is unknown. Perhaps the Seminoles only saw the plantation being used as a base for military operations, and that its destruction would help their

cause. Soon after the burning of Bulow Ville, the young planter John Bulow sailed to Paris where he died of unknown causes shortly thereafter.
As for King Philip, he was captured in September 1836, at the ruins of
the Dunlawton Plantation, surprised by soldiers at first light. "We soon
found ourselves unexpectedly in the presence of royalty," wrote Jacob
Motte, "for there stood King Philip the principal chief on the St. John's
River naked as he was born, except the breech-cloth; and covered with
most unkingly dirt." The chief had been knocked down by a charging
horseman. "Though a captive," Motte continued, "there was still a stern-
ness in this chief's dark eye,—which black as a thundercloud and emit-
ting flashes like its lightning,—plainly told his spirit was unquelled."

With his father imprisoned, Coacoochee (Wildcat) and other leaders were summoned by runners. Motte described Coacoochee as "the
Napoleon of the Seminoles; and his safe keeping was a matter of much
consequence, for his influence among his people was even greater than
that of his father." Motte described Cooacoochee's appearance as having
"all the pomp of scarlet and burnished silver; his head decorated with a
plume of white crane feathers, and a silver band around his gaudy turban. His leather leggings were also superceded by a pair of bright scarlet
cloth. He insisted upon being mounted on a spirited horse; and attired
in his picturesque native costume, he rode with a great deal of savage
grace and majesty."

Army leaders convinced Coacoochee to bring in other Seminole
leaders for peace talks, whereupon they were captured under flags of
truce and imprisoned in St. Augustine. This brings us to the next stop
along the Seminole Trail.

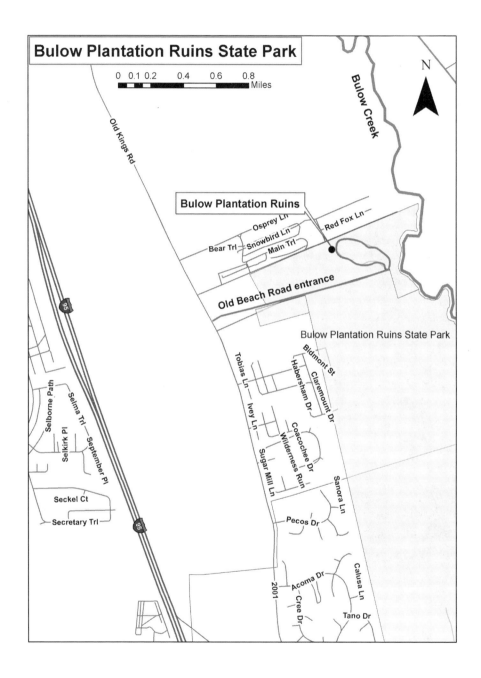

The Old Beach Road entrance to Bulow Plantation Ruins Historic State Park.

Getting There

The access roads to Bulow Plantation Ruins Historic State Park are some of the most scenic in Florida. First, if coming from Daytona Beach, you must travel north along the canopied Kings Highway with its centuries-old arching live oaks. The road was first built by the Spanish to connect St. Augustine to southern communities such as New Smyrna. Along the way, you'll pass the ruins of another nineteenth-century sugar mill destroyed by Seminoles, the Dummett Mill, as you pass through Bulow Creek State Park. A short ways north of the mill site, you can stop and stand in awe at the Fairchild Oak, one of the largest live oaks in the South. It was a notable tree even when Seminole Indians lived in the area.

To reach Bulow Ruins from the Kings Highway, you have to turn east down "the Old Beach Road," a canopied unpaved road that was the original entrance to the Bulow Plantation, and little has changed. A tight canopy of palms, live oaks, sweetgum, and other hardwoods provides cool shade. It doesn't get much better. The road is only one wagon width wide, so drive slowly and use one of several pullover spots to allow oncoming vehicles to pass. It is easy to picture slow-moving wagons transporting sugar, molasses, and rum from the plantation.

Turning into the state park, the first view is of scenic Bulow Creek, where you can launch a canoe or kayak for a leisurely paddle. The creek, connecting to the Halifax River, was used to ship goods to and from the plantation by water. You can either hike a quarter mile to the ruins from here or drive a circular trail to a small parking area closer to the ruins. Several other nature trails branch off from there. The park is open from 9 a.m. to 5 p.m. Thursdays through Mondays; closed Tuesdays and Wednesdays. To learn more, log onto http://www.floridastateparks.org/bulowplantation/. The address is County Road 2001, Flagler Beach, Florida, 32110.

Other historic sugar mill sites destroyed by Seminoles in the re-

Moss and ruins of the Bulow Sugar Mill in Bulow Plantation Ruins Historic State Park.

gion include the Dunlawton Plantation Sugar Mill Ruins. Listed on the National Register of Historic Places in 1973, it later became a botanical gardens owned by Volusia County, now called Historic Dunlawton Sugar Mill Gardens. The site includes stone ruins and interpretive signs along with ancient trees, colorful landscaping, and large concrete sculptures. It is open daily from 8 a.m. to seasonally adjusted evening times seven days a week and is located in Port Orange, one mile west of US 1 off Herbert Street on Sugar Mill Road. The address is 950 Old Sugar Mill Road, Port Orange, 32129. For more information, log onto http://www.dunlawtonsugarmillgardens.org/ or call (386) 767-1735.

Ruins of the Cruger and DePeyster Sugar Mill, now known as the New Smyrna Sugar Mill, are also open to the public. Seminoles destroyed the mill only five years after it was built and the site was later used by soldiers during the war. The address is 1050 Old Mission Road, New Smyrna Beach, 32168. It is open during daylight hours 365 days a years; (904) 428-2125.

Eight

The Great Escape

Fort Marion

*When King Philip, Coacoochee, Osceola, and other Seminole leaders were captured under white flags of truce, it largely put an end to the raiding of plantations along Florida's northeast coast. But what followed was undoubtedly one of the greatest escapes in United States history. The Seminole Trail takes us to Castillo de San Marcos in St. Augustine, what the Americans called **Fort Marion** during their occupation.*

"I was one of the party sent out to meet Osceola when he was coming to St. Augustine under a flag of truce. … No sooner was he safe within our lines than the order to seize him, kill if necessary, was given, and one of the soldiers knocked him down with the butt of his musket. He was then bound and we brought him to Fort Marion and he was put in the dungeon. We were all outraged by the cowardly way he was betrayed into being captured."—John S. Masters, a soldier during the war, quoted in *The Seminoles of Florida* by Minnie Moore-Willson

"There were some individuals who pretended to condemn the capture of Osceola and his warriors as dishonorable on the part of Gen. Jesup;— as a base violation of a flag of truce. Tis true they had a white flag flying; but they were never told that it would afford them indemnity from capture on this occasion. On the contrary, they had been repeatedly told that the only terms with which they could be received were those of actual surrender and that no flag would be received on any other terms. Indeed, there was too much sympathy extended upon these treacherous, murderous savages."—Jacob Rhett Motte, surgeon during the Second Seminole War

Sobering. That's the best way to describe the clammy stone cell of Castillo de San Marcos in St. Augustine, called Fort Marion after the Americans took control from Spain in 1821 (though the name was changed back in the mid twentieth century). While most modern-day visitors pose for photos beside cannons, mortars, and living history interpreters dressed as soldiers, take a moment to enter the dank room along the southwest side of the fort to study the former cells that housed Seminole leaders Osceola, Coacoochee, and several others captured under flags of truce in 1837.

The block walls, carved from coquina limestone bedrock in the late 1600s and early1700s, are several feet thick. The floors are stone, and the ceilings are stone, too. The cell door leads to the interior square of the fort, so only a tiny window six inches wide and eighteen inches high about eighteen feet above the floor leads to the outside and freedom. It's easy to imagine what this window represented to a freedom-loving people accustomed to the open air of Florida.

Besides Coacoochee and Osceola, one of the imprisoned warriors included John Horse, also known as John Cavallo or Gopher John, per-

Giant door of Fort San Marcos in St. Augustine.

haps the most notable Black Seminole during the war. He often acted as a military advisor to Osceola and other leaders and chiefs. Horse would later be relocated to Indian Territory (Oklahoma), but when Black Seminoles were at risk of being forced into slavery, he led his family and a large contingent of Black Seminoles to Mexico, where they found freedom and often served as border guards. After the Civil War, Horse moved back across the border and worked as an Army scout in Texas before returning to Mexico. Descendants of Black Seminoles still reside in northern Mexico.

The purpose of capturing and imprisoning these Seminole leaders in Fort Marion was simple—break the spirit of the Seminole resistance. John Jacob Motte, a surgeon during the Second Seminole War, describes the reasoning in his war diary: "The capture of these chiefs we knew would by no means increase the friendly feelings of the Indians towards us, but would tend rather to render them more vindictive and desperate than ever; and it was therefore expected by many that there would still be some hard fighting. Though we expected to have a few months more of hard service, the existing state of affairs at this time, we thought, most evidently tended to bring about an early termination to this disastrous war."

The soldiers, however, didn't foresee the ingenuity and desperation of their Seminole prisoners. A plan of escape was developed. With a contraband knife, Coacoochee was able to drive it into the cement grout of the west wall and climb up to a small ledge before the window. From there, he studied the window's size and the bars that lay across it. One of the bars was rusty from age, and after diligent work, he was able to loosen it. That still left a small opening for a man to climb through. For escape to succeed, each person would have to become smaller, and that meant fasting.

Fasting was nothing new to the Seminoles. Participants in the annual Green Corn Ceremony often fasted for four or more days to purify mind, body, and spirit. Fasting served to starve the body and feed the soul, according to Muscogee and Seminole beliefs. And in this case, fasting was a means of gaining freedom. The Seminoles were also able to obtain certain herbs that aided in the purification process, and maybe some other things came into play as well. Some say it was Seminole magic. Perhaps Coacoochee, or a shaman in the group, used magic to put the guard to sleep and shrink their bodies to slip between the bars of the tiny window of their cell and climb down the stone walls to freedom.

The Seminoles did have their shamans or makers of medicine, as did most Native American tribes, and magic was said to be used by Seminoles in fighting enemies that had superior numbers and firepower. Each war leader was said to have a shaman helping his band. Seminole war chief and medicine man *Arpeika*, or Sam Jones, for example, was often blamed—or given credit for—the sudden death of soldiers' horses.

"They [sorcerers] could make tracks and trails invisible, ruin the nose of a bloodhound, and change into a bear and run swiftly to safety with children on their back," wrote Brent Weisman in *Unconquered People*. "The sorcerers could make themselves invisible or impervious to pain or the effects of bullets.... Magic songs were used to protect the Seminoles when they parlayed with the soldiers. Many objects in the Seminole medicine bundles are meant to give power in war, particularly by casting spells over the soldiers or by shielding the people from harm. Clearly the Seminoles used everything in their power to keep the military at bay, but the United States was just as determined in its will to remove the Indians."

Coacoochee doesn't refer directly to magic in his account of the escape, nor would he have likely mentioned it to outsiders if it was used. He does mention an undisclosed herb used in helping them reduce their size since, as one Seminole man asserted, all the fasting in the world cannot reduce the size of a person's skull. In his own words, here is Coacoochee's account of one of the great escapes in United States military history:

> We had been growing sickly from day to day in a small room, eighteen or twenty feet square. Light came through a hold eighteen feet from the floor. Through this was our escape or remain and die.
>
> A sentinel was constantly at the door. From our bed the hole looked small, but if we could get our heads through, we believed we should have no difficulty. To reach the hole was the first object. From time to time we cut up the forage-bags allowed us to sleep on and made them into ropes. I could reach the hole when standing upon the shoulders of my partner, and worked a knife into a crevice of the stonework as far as I could reach. Upon this I raised myself to the aperture, which I found that with some reduction of person, I could get through.

In order to reduce ourselves, we took medicine, five days. Under the pretext of being sick we were permitted to obtain the roots required. For some weeks we watched the moon, that the night of our attempt should be dark. We commenced the medicine calculating the entire disappearance of the moon.

The prison keeper on the night determined, annoyed us frequently coming into the room talking and singing. We first thought of tying him and putting his head in a bag so that should he call for assistance, he could not be heard. Then we pretended to be asleep, and when he returned paid him no regard. This accomplished our object. He came in, and went out immediately. We could hear him snore near the door.

I then took a rope, hidden under our bed, mounted my comrade's shoulders, raised myself to the knife, and reached the embrasure. Here I made fast the rope, so that my friend might follow me. I then passed through enough rope to reach the ditch fifty feet outside. I had calculated the distance when going for roots. With difficulty I got my head through, for sharp stones took off the skin of my breast and back. My head through first, I went down head-foremost until my feet were through, fearing every moment the rope would break.

Safely on the ground, I awaited Talmus for whom, in the event of discovery, he was to pull another rope passed through the hole. The night was very dark. Two men passed near me, talking, and I could see them distinctly. Soon I heard Talmus above me. His head was through, but his body would come no farther. I urged him to throw out his breath. Soon he came tumbling down. For a few mo-

Small window in cell at Fort San Marcos through which Seminole prisoners escaped. At the time, the fort was known as Fort Marion.

Wall that the escaping Seminole prisoners had to climb down from the tiny window through which they escaped.

ments I thought him dead. I dragged him to water close by which restored him, but his leg was so lame, he was unable to walk. I carried him to a scrub near town. Daylight was just breaking. It was evident we must move rapidly.

I caught a mule in the field, made a bridle from my sash, mounted my companion, and started for the St. Johns. The mule was used one day, but fearing the whites would track us, we felt more secure in the hammock, moving very slow.

We continued five days, eating roots and berries, then joined my band at the head of the Tomoka River near the Atlantic.

Osceola was asked to join them, but he was too sick with malaria. He was moved the next month to Fort Moultrie, South Carolina, where he died on January 31, 1838, and was characterized as a Seminole martyr in the popular press. His head, however, would be removed from his body by the attending physician, Frederick Weedon, supposedly for study, and hasn't been seen since a museum fire in 1866.

Coacoochee's escape reinvigorated the Seminole resistance. No one could trust the white generals. The only option was to fight and to withdraw deeper into the Florida swamps. "I would rather be killed by a white man in Florida than die in Arkansas," Wildcat is quoted to have said.

Eventually, Coacoochee was captured, in 1841, only because his young daughter—his only child—was captured first. The commander of federal troops at the time, General Worth, guessed correctly that he had found the war leader's Achilles heel. Wildcat agreed to talk peace with the general, and upon seeing his child, his dignified bearing was said to fail as he was overcome with emotion. His speech to General Worth also revealed his deep feelings for Florida and for his people:

The whites dealt unjustly with me. I came to them when they deceived me. I loved the land I was upon. My body is made of its sands. The Great Spirit gave me legs to walk over it, eyes to see it, hands to aid myself, a head with which I think. The sun which shines warm and bright brings forth our crops, and the moon brings back spirits of our warriors, our feathers, our wives, and our children. The white man comes, he grows pale and sickly; why can we not live in peace? They steal our horses and cattle, cheat us and take our lands. They may shoot us, chain our hands and feet, but the red man's heart will be free. I have come to you in peace, and have taken you by the hand. I will sleep in your camp, though your soldiers stand around me thick as pine trees. I am done. When we know each other better, I will say more.

Wildcat's surrender and eventual promise to emigrate to the West prompted band after weary band to follow suit. "As vessel after vessel anchored in Tampa Bay to carry these wronged and persecuted people to their distant homes, the cruelty of the undertaking was apparent to the most callous heart," wrote Minnie Moore-Willson in the 1911 edition of the classic *The Seminoles of Florida*. "With lingering looks the Seminoles saw the loved scenes of their childhood fade away. The wails and anguish of those heart-broken people, as the ships left the shores, touched the hearts of the most hardened sailor."

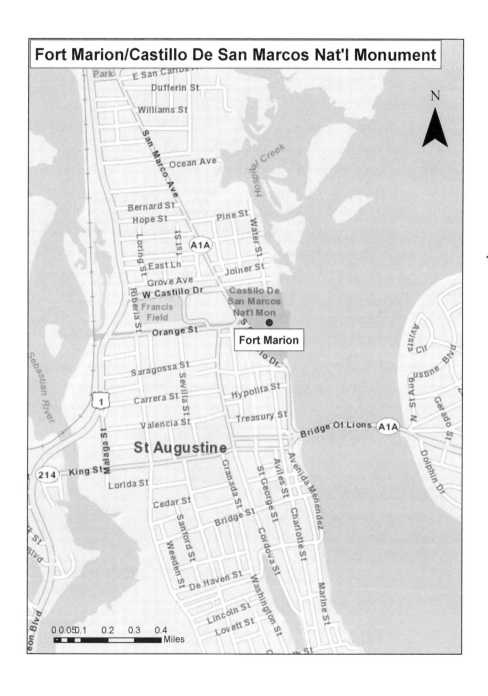

Fort Marion/Castillo De San Marcos Nat'l Monument

Getting There

Castillo de San Marcos National Monument, located in downtown St. Augustine along the Intracoastal Waterway, is open every day except Christmas from 8:45 a.m. to 4:45 p.m. From I-95, take Exit 318 (Route 16) and head east following signs to the St. Augustine Historic Sites and Downtown. Turn right onto US 1 and travel about one mile and turn left onto West Castillo Drive. Turn right at the next traffic light and you'll see the monument and parking ahead on the left. There is both a parking and entrance fee. Self-guided tour brochures are available in several languages, and park rangers give interpretive talks throughout the day. Re-enactors in period dress can be seen around the fort, and they often give periodic presentations and historic weapons demonstrations. For more information, log onto http://www.nps.gov/casa/index.htm. The address is 1 South Castillo Drive, St. Augustine, FL 32084; (904) 829-6506.

Nine
Florida's Pickett's Charge

Battle of Okeechobee

*Coacoochee's escape from Fort Marion reinvigorated the Seminole cause at a time when most of the remaining Seminoles in Florida were being driven farther south into the peninsula. Along the northern shores of Lake Okeechobee, the Seminoles decided to make a stand in what would become the largest battle of the Second Seminole War. The Seminole Trail takes us just east of present-day Okeechobee to the **Okeechobee Battlefield**.*

"The first reenactment I did was the most exciting," said Pedro Zepeda of the Big Cypress Seminole Reservation. "I was fourteen and I was running and dodging imaginary bullets. It's still fun and exciting to do." Zepeda, now 28, sported a trimmed beard and moustache and long dark hair in a ponytail. Dressed in period Seminole clothes and moc-casins, he held his tiger maple reproduction musket and wiped sweat from his brow. It was unusually hot and muggy for early February, even for the northern shore of Lake Okeechobee. After all, most of the na-tion was enduring a record snowfall. But Zepeda and a small band of Seminole reenactors still put on a spirited fight against men portraying soldiers and Missouri Volunteers for the 2011 reenactment of the Battle of Okeechobee.

The annual event was held on a 145-acre chunk of state land that is not yet open to the public on a regular basis. The Florida Park Service has adopted a multi-year management plan to restore pastureland to a more natural state and to remove exotic plants. Depending on funding, public facilities will be built along with an interpretive trail, interactive sites, and a pavilion. One day, the Okeechobee Battlefield Historic State Park will be open year-round.

The reenactment, smaller than the long established annual event at the Dade Battlefield Historic State Park, is no less significant since it ob-serves the largest battle of the Second Seminole War. In 1837, General Thomas Jesup had nine thousand men at his disposal—the largest force of the war—which he divided into seven columns. Colonel Zachary Taylor would take more than a thousand of those men and march south along the Kissimmee River in an effort to engage or capture Seminoles. Almost immediately, he captured Jumper and 63 followers. The next day, 26 more Seminoles were brought in. It was clear Taylor was on the trail of a large band of fleeing Seminoles.

As was the practice during the war, Taylor set up small forts and supply depots about a day's march apart and pared off men to cover them. By the time he neared the oceanlike Lake Okeechobee—which didn't even show up on his poor map—he still had about eight hundred men. It was here, on Christmas Day, that he encountered a Seminole warrior tending horses in what was likely a ruse. When pressed as to the location of the main body of Seminoles, the warrior pointed across an open stretch of four- to five-foot-high sawgrass to a wide tree-covered rise. The lakeside hammock—a natural fortress—was the perfect location for an outnumbered foe to make a stand.

The Seminoles were not only led by Arpeika (a.k.a. Sam Jones)—who would later be the main holdout in the Everglades—and Alligator, but also by Wildcat and the Black Seminole John Horse, two leaders General Jesup had captured under a flag of truce but who had miraculously escaped from Fort Marion in St. Augustine only a short time before (see Chapter Eight). It is safe to assume that the two had a score to settle. In all, the Seminole force consisted of around four hundred warriors. They were backed by one of the most powerful medicine men of the time, on par or greater than Sam Jones himself—Otolke-Thlocko, commonly referred to as The Prophet. He drummed and chanted to inspire the red and black warriors, and to help them become immune to bullets. Surely he helped to paint their faces—mostly red and black for war and death. The Seminoles were primed and ready for a fully pitched battle. Many had good rifles, likely of Cuban/Spanish origin, unlike the shorter range muskets of most of the Americans.

By order of Taylor, the initial charge through the waterlogged razor-sharp sawgrass was by the hapless Missouri Volunteers, led by Colonel Richard Gentry. They had begun their journey to Florida by boat with six hundred men, but a yellow fever outbreak in New Orleans, coupled with the difficult conditions of the voyage, prompted 150 to desert. Then, a hurricane hit the overloaded boats carrying their horses and most of the mounts perished, dashing the men's hopes of being a feared cavalry unit. More than half of the remaining men then headed back home, leaving about 150 to slog through the Florida jungle with Taylor in search of a stealthy foe. Near Lake Okeechobee, they found the main Seminole body. Colonel Gentry wanted to flank the entrenched Seminoles, believing that a frontal assault across the marsh would provide the Seminoles with easy targets. Colonel Taylor listened to his plan, then brusquely asked, "Colonel Gentry, are you *afraid* to attack the center through the swamp?"

Gentry stiffened and willfully followed Taylor's orders. He joined his volunteers in wading through the thick mud of the sawgrass flat toward a concealed enemy in what most knew would be a suicidal frontal assault. Taylor's regulars stood in the rear and watched while other columns moved in behind the volunteers. "The decision to send in raw troops to bear the first brunt of battle, almost as a sacrifice to open the way for the Regulars, was just one of those difficult choices that often face a field commander," wrote historian J. Floyd Monk about the battle. "For the first time in the war—perhaps the only time—the commander [Taylor] knew almost exactly what he was up against. It would be like storming a medieval fortress, across a moat, and it would be brutal."

Militia reenactors fire muskets at the 2011 Battle of Okeechobee Reenactment.

To make it easier to shoot the soldiers, the Seminoles had carefully cleared low palmettos and tall sawgrass in an area in front of the hammock, removing any chance for cover. They also knew thick mud would slow the advance. In many places, the sucking mud and water was waist deep. When the volunteers approached to within a hundred yards, Seminole sharpshooters—many of them in trees and draped in Spanish moss—opened fire. As was the Seminole tactic, officers were targeted first. Five officers were wounded in less than a minute, causing disarray among some of the men. The advance of the Missouri Volunteers was the Seminole War version of Picket's charge at Gettysburg.

Gentry ordered his men to squat low in the grass while he tried to regroup his decimated forces. Men wallowed forward in the mud and tried to conceal themselves in the sparse sawgrass, but Seminole marksmen in treetops could still spot them and the firing continued. Ascertaining that his only hope was to gain the protection of the hammock, he ordered a charge: "Come on, boys! We're almost there; charge into the hammock!" While some men bolted from the fighting, the majority gathered behind Gentry. A small group reached the hammock's edge whereupon Gentry was shot at point-blank range. His son, a sergeant-major, was simultaneously shot in the wrist, possibly by the same bullet. Seeking to inspire his men, Gentry ordered that he be lifted to his feet. "Fight on," he screamed, "till the foe retreats!"

Small skirmishes erupted from within the hammock. Captain Cornelius Gilliam described the Seminole mode of combat in the close quarters: "The Seminole manner of fighting was advantageous to themselves. ... When closely pressed on they ran; these would hide and fire again [before advancing to their former positions]." More than twenty volunteers were killed in the battle, and Gentry would not live to see another sunrise.

With the volunteer charge waning, Taylor ordered the Sixth Infantry's five companies to attack. Dressed in period blue woolen trousers and jackets and tall leather forage hats, they made easy targets. Additionally, as in the Dade Battle, many of the men wore white shoulder straps that made an X pattern across the chest as if a bull's-eye were painted there for Seminole sharpshooters.

Immediately, officers began to fall, among them Colonel Ramsey Thompson. Propped against a tree facing the foe, hit by three different musket balls, Thompson called out his last orders, "Keep steady men, charge the hammock—remember the regiment to which you belong!" The Sixth Infantry suffered nearly forty percent casualties, and one company had only four men who were not wounded, and all of its officers had been killed.

"The enemy was posted in the strongest position that I have ever seen in Florida," wrote Lieutenant Robert C. Buchanan of the Fourth Infantry in his journal. "He was in an immense hammock on the borders of Lake Okeechobee, having, at the point where we penetrated it, a saw-grass swamp three quarters of a mile wide and several miles long. The mud in the swamp was knee-deep, and we were completely tired out before we reached the hammock."

After the fighting had raged for almost three hours, a bayonet charge was formed with remnants of six companies and volunteers and about 160 men of the Fourth Infantry. They gained the hammock and forced the Indians towards the lake, while fresh reserves began to flank the Indians on the right side. Before retreating, the Seminoles employed one last act of deception. In the close hammock fighting, some of the soldiers confused Seminoles with friendly Delaware Indians, prompting Colonel William Foster to call out, "Are you Delaware?"

"Yes, Delaware! Delaware!" the Seminoles cried.

The soldiers hesitated long enough for the Seminoles to fire another deadly volley which, according to Foster, "caused more injury than all the others during the fight."

The Seminoles retreated to the east and eventually moved across the lake in dugout canoes. Some of the reserves pursued them until nightfall, but the main Seminole force escaped. Their main goals for the battle were achieved—allow for the escape of their women and children and inflict as many casualties as possible, thereby halting Taylor's advance through their country. "In fact the men were so much jaded," wrote Lieutenant Buchanan soon after the battle, "that it was with the utmost difficulty they could bring out the bodies of the dead."

There was no clear winner of the Battle of Okeechobee. The Seminoles inflicted the larger number of casualties—26 killed and 112 wounded among Taylor's forces compared to the Seminoles' 11 killed and 14 wounded. Taylor speculated in his report that the Seminoles "probably suffered ... equally with ourselves, they having left ten dead on the ground ... doubtless carrying off many more, as is customary with them, when practicable." Later, Coacoochee would dispute Taylor's assertion and provide the official numbers for Seminole dead and wounded. Taylor's losses would rank among the highest in all of the Indian battles.

While the dead from Taylor's forces were buried on dry ground next to the battlefield, the Seminole dead were left where they fell, much like Dade's men two years earlier. "First went to the camp where are the graves of the killed," wrote Lieutenant Henry Prince on February 7, 1838, six weeks after the battle. "Then crossed the saw-grass quagmire—then through the compact cypress swamp to the shore or beach of the great Lake which lay before me like the ocean in a calm. No land was in sight from left to right. The bodies of Indians were mouldering here and there near the trees where [they] fell."

Scholars point out that the Seminoles were only defeated by Napoleonic standards—they retreated from the disputed ground—and since most American officers followed these standards, Taylor claimed victory. Heroic descriptions of the battle were released to the public, descriptions which may have been exaggerated since some in Taylor's command, such as Lt. Colonel William S. Foster, took issue with his

Seminole reenactors clear guns after the 2011 Battle of Okeechobee Reenactment.

report. Still, Taylor soon became a brigadier general, and his stature on the political horizon was greatly enhanced. He was perhaps the only American war leader who left the Second Seminole War with an enhanced reputation. After successes in the Mexican War, Taylor rode his fame to the White House as the twelfth president of the United States.

Of the Missouri Volunteers, Taylor wrote that they broke and ran soon after the Seminoles started shooting—"nor could they be again brought into action as a body." His report reflected the long-standing tension between regulars and citizen volunteers, best summarized by Jacob Motte in his *Journey into Wilderness*: "When will Congress awake to the worse than useless squandering of the public money in the employment of these useless and unwieldy hordes of unorganized militia! The country has suffered often enough by the inefficiency and undisciplined volunteers, to say nothing of the great and useless expense attending the support of them for only short periods. In action they have seldom done anything. In Col. Taylor's battle, it was reported on good authority, that the volunteers fled the field after the first fire; leaving their commander to perish alone, while the Regulars manfully stood the brunt of the fight. …"

Taylor's account was hotly contested by surviving members of the volunteers. Missouri senator Thomas Hart Benton lashed out at Taylor's report on the Senate floor: "No allowance was made for undisciplined troops who had faced a terrible danger—who had lost their command-er—who had suffered severely—who had their killed and wounded friends to take care of—who had discretionary orders to retreat—and who saw two hundred regulars idle as a reserve." Hearings were also held on the matter by the Missouri Legislature. Taylor's report, however, was backed by the Secretary of War and little could change it.

In reality, both sides in the dispute were partially correct. Some volunteers did retreat after the initial volleys and refused to rejoin the fray, while others bravely followed their leader, Colonel Gentry, into the hammock.

Less than two months after the Battle of Okeechobee, with the Seminoles fleeing deep into the Everglades and Big Cypress, General Thomas Jesup wrote to Secretary of War Joel Roberts Poinsett with this recommendation: "In regard to the Seminoles, we have committed the error of attempting to remove them when their lands were not required for agricultural purposes; when they were not in the way of white inhab-itants; and when the greater portion of their country was an unexplored wilderness. … My decided opinion is, that unless immediate emigration be abandoned, the war will continue for years to come, and at constantly accumulating expense."

Jesup felt that if the Seminoles were lulled into a peace treaty and settled into one identifiable location, they could more easily be rounded up and relocated west at a later date. His recommendation was soundly

Seminole Indian Pedro Zepeda at the 2011 Battle of Okeechobee Reenactment.

rejected by Poinsett, and the Second Seminole War dragged on for several more years, just as Jesup had feared. But never again could the Seminoles mount as large a force in one location as they did at the Battle of Okeechobee.

Before the state purchased the Okeechobee battlefield site, or what was left of it after roads and development had encroached on all sides, it was considered one of America's eleven most endangered historic sites by the National Trust for Historic Preservation. Enter a locally formed group called the Okeechobee Battlefield Friends. In 1987 they organized the 150th anniversary reenactment of the battle to raise public awareness of the site. Bob Carr of the Archaeological and Historical Conservancy of Miami and Becky Williamson of Okeechobee were leaders of the effort. The expanse of sawgrass on the site had long been turned into improved pasture, but enough of the original battlefield remained undeveloped to warrant protection. In 2006, state representative Richard Machek persuaded the Florida Legislature to purchase 145 acres of the site for $3.2 million. With the money allocated, the proposed purchase was brought before Governor Jeb Bush and the Florida Cabinet.

"When I walked into the cabinet room it was so impressive because large portraits of Indian warriors surrounded the room," said Okeechobee councilman and reenactor Dowling Watford in *Okeechobee* magazine. "It just felt so appropriate. I felt like their spirit was watching us preserve a part of the battlefield. It was a moving and emotional experience—one of the highest highs I've ever had in my life."

Hurricanes cancelled some of the reenactments, but they resumed in 2008 at the new park. Through mini grants given to teachers, fourth-grade students visit the site on Fridays before the reenactment to witness various historical demonstrations and learn about the battle. Home schoolers, private school classes, and members of the Seminole Tribe of Florida also take part. "This is a passion of ours," said Harvard Burney, a volunteer Seminole reenactor from Fanning Springs who was joined by his wife, Laney, at the reenactment. "We've done this for a dozen years and when we [reenactors] come together, we're like a family. We love the history and enjoy talking about it to school kids and the general public. We try to tie it in with what's going on now, comparing then and now. People get interested and they want to know more."

Laney added, "There are many different facets to events in history. The 'winner' usually writes the books. We hope we inspire someone to go out and learn more."

The Burneys displayed examples of Seminole foods, including Seminole pumpkin, turnips, hickory nuts, bananas, and wild oranges. Harvard Burney, who believes he has Muscogee blood on his mother's side, feels a resonance with Seminole ways. "When I first went to Big Cypress [Seminole reservation], I felt like I had come home."

The annual reenactments are a way for the two sides represented at the battle to join together. At the 2010 reenactment, Vero Beach resident Matt Taylor, great-great-great-grandson of Colonel Zachary Taylor, and Willie Johns, a descendant of the great Seminole war leader Coacoochee, met for the first time. Taylor showed off a black powder pistol that belonged to his famous ancestor, on loan from a Louisiana museum. Peacefully, under the Florida sun, Taylor and Johns watched reenactors portray their ancestors during one of the most heated battles in Florida's

Seminole reenactor Harvard Burney at the 2011 Battle of Okeechobee Reenactment.

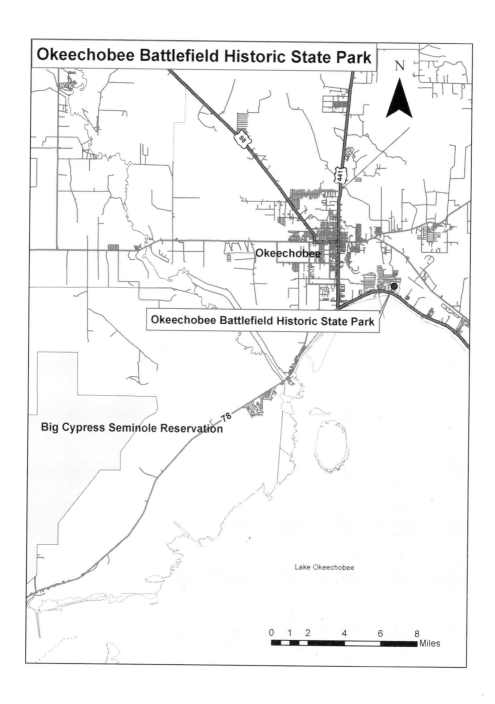

history.

Getting There

From Florida's east coast: Take 70 West to intersection of 70 and 441 in Okeechobee City; turn left onto 441 South and continue through Okeechobee to 441 S.E.; turn left onto 441 S.E. and go approximately 1 mile and look for signage. From West Palm Beach: Take 710 (also known as Bee Line Highway) to 70 West; take 70 West to intersection of 70 and 441 in Okeechobee City; turn left onto 441 South and continue through Okeechobee to 441 S.E.; turn left onto 441 S.E. and go approximately one mile and look for signage. The address is 3500 S.E. 38th Ave., Okeechobee, FL 34974. For more information, call (863) 634-9587 or (863) 484-0998 or visit www.okeechobeebattlefield.com

Ten
Night Raid!

Indian Key

*The Seminole Trail dips south to **Indian Key** in the Florida Keys. Here, Seminole leader Chakaika and seventeen canoe loads of warriors landed at night to raid the island's settlement. They made away with a huge storehouse of goods and killed horticulturist Henry Perrine and several others.*

I solated off the mainland near Lower Matacumbe Key, about halfway between Cape Florida and Key West, the settlers on 12-acre Indian Key generally felt safe during the Second Seminole War. The colony's founder, Jacob Housman, made his fortune salvaging shipwrecks off the treacherous reefs a few miles offshore, and he started a trading post on the island for coastal vessels and for Seminole Indians before hostilities broke out. He was never held in high regard by the Seminoles, however,

Indian Key, site of a Seminole raid in 1840 in which Dr. Henry Perrine was killed.

and was often considered "unethical" in several of his dealings with others, too.

During the Second Seminole War, in 1839, Housman proposed that the government pay him $200 a head to capture or kill Indians in South Florida. The proposal eventually reached the ears of Seminole leaders in the region, likely through slaves or Cuban fishermen. The government didn't take the offer seriously, but the Seminoles did.

Despite his soiled reputation, Housman did have some political influence. He managed to have Dade County created and successfully made Indian Key its first county seat. Housman organized a militia to protect the island, dirt embankments were constructed, and a half dozen cannons were stationed at key locations. The island's inhabitants also solicited the support of the United States government in 1837: "the peculiar Situation of Indian Key renders it liable to incursions from these hostile savages more than any other location on the coast; the temptation too is considerable inasmuch as a large store is kept on the key which is at all times filled with provisions and munitions of war for the use of the inhabitants and wreckers engaged on the coast, and these facts are well known to the Indians, they having previous to the breaking out of hostilities been in the habit of trading at this store."

As a result of the request, a naval revenue cutter began using Indian Key as a base along with elements of the Florida Squadron. But the soldiers moved to nearby Tea Table Key in the spring of 1840.

In 1838, horticulturist Henry Perrine and his family arrived at Indian Key from New York to settle into the community of four or five families, feeling safer on the island than on the mainland due to Indian depredations. Dr. Perrine set up a nursery to propagate tropical agricultural plants such as yam, ginger, agave, Sisal hemp, cassava, indigo, sugar cane, pimento, tea, orange, shaddock, grapefruit, lime, citron, sugar apple, banana, plantain, pineapple, coconut, sapodilla, soursop, avocado, mango, mamey sapota, boxwood, white mulberry, and various spices and medicinal herbs. Swarms of stingless bees from the Yucatan were brought in as well.

"I cannot forget our delight on first seeing this beautiful little island of only 12 acres," wrote Henry Perrine's daughter, Hester Perrine Walker, several years later. "It was truly a 'Gem of the Ocean.' The trees were many of them covered with morning glories of all colors, while the waving palms, tamarinds, papaws, guavas, seaside grape trees and many others too numerous to mention made it seem to us like fairy land, coming as we did from the midst of snow and ice."

Life was generally peaceful on Indian Key in the balmy Keys weather, with the main threat being possible hurricanes during the warm months. But in the wee hours of August 7, 1840, another deadly force threatened the island inhabitants. Seventeen canoe loads of Seminoles, locally called "Spanish Indians" due to their knowledge of the Spanish language—likely from trading with Cuban fishermen—landed on the

Indian Key trail.

island after paddling thirty miles from the mainland. They were led by Chakaika (spelled various ways), an imposing six-footer who sought no compromise with whites during the war. He had already gained some renown for a surprise attack on a post of Army soldiers headed by Colonel William S. Harney at a trading post along the Caloosahatchee River. Most of the soldiers had been killed and Harney escaped "with only drawers and shirt." It is believed that Chakaika's band may have included descendants of the once powerful Calusa tribe, and some were of mixed Spanish heritage.

It was apparent that Chakaika or men in his raiding party knew the island well because, according to a naval investigator afterwards, "the Indians were conducted to this attack by some person or persons acquainted with the localities of the Key, … [because] their landing was effected on the outside of the Key, at a point most remote from their approach, yet at a corner of the town uninhabited, whilst every consideration, if ignorant of this fact, would have induced them to have landed at a point directly opposite." Also, a large naval force led by Lieutenant Rogers had left the island the day before, leaving only five sailors. "That his departure was communicated to or looked for by the Indians, there cannot be a doubt," the investigator concluded.

Chakaika's plan was to wait until dawn to attack in daylight, but a wakeful carpenter named James Glass discovered the band. He and a neighbor alerted Housman and other inhabitants. While the discovered Seminoles rushed their attack in darkness around two or three in the morning, many settlers hid in bushes or rock crevasses or escaped by boat.

Hester Perrine Walker, a sixteen-year-old at the time of the raid, described the attack on her house and hiding with her mother and siblings in a small, water-filled "turtle crawl" or cellar beneath the house that stored live turtles for eventual consumption:

We were aroused from our sleep by the terrific war whoop, simultaneously with the crack of rifles and the falling of the glass from our broken windows," she wrote. "I saw this terrific crowd of Indians dancing and whooping like demons by the flash of their rifles.

My father told us to go down into the bath room, and 'he would see what he could do.' With a martyr's heroism, he went out upon the piazza, and called to them in Spanish, 'I am a physician and will go with you to heal your people.'

Upon this they gave a great shout and left the house. Father came down then and closed the trap door, telling us to 'go into the narrow passageway, for if we remained in the cellar, the Indians might see us through the opening.' He then drew a heavy chest of seeds over the door, concealing every trace of its existence.

He had scarcely accomplished this when the Indians returned and with their tomahawks commenced battering down the door and breaking in the windows, having apparently given up their intention of sparing him. Father fled to the cupola, we think, hoping that he might be able from there to see help coming from the Naval depot, and that, as the door was a heavy one, he might be able to hold out until relief came. For a few moments as they swarmed up the stairs after him, there was a horrid silence, only broken by the blows of their tomahawks upon the door, then a crash, one wild shriek, a rifle shot, and all was still.

They then came down and commenced pillaging our house. ... As they went into our pantry for a short space there was again silence, as they consumed the good things there. After their repast was over, they would take first one pile of dishes and then another, and throw them upon the floor, breaking them to pieces, and they would dance and whoop. So they broke everything in the house before they set fire to it.

There was no wind and it burned slowly. Soon after daylight the smoke began to come slowly into our hiding place. The tide had risen until there was only room for our heads between the water and the boards, but when it was low there was perhaps a foot in depth. Remember that this hiding place was only four feet wide, four feet high and ten feet long. Then the bank sloped gradually until at the end of the wharf it was about ten or twelve feet, up to the trap door. On the end of this wharf about six cords of wood were piled waiting for the wrecking vessels to take it off. Toward ten o'clock (as we thought) the smoke became so annoying that we were obliged to throw water over our heads to be able to breathe.

The Indians heard us, and coming down to the trap door, lifted it and looked down, their shadow upon the water being distinctly visible to us. Had they turned their heads in the slightest they would have seen us, but seeing the numbers of turtles splashing around, they must have supposed the noise they heard was from them.

The smoke and steam became unendurable. The piazza fell in and the flames communicated to the boards over our heads, but we kept them subdued for a while by throwing water upon them, but when the wharf beyond us and the cords of wood upon it were all in flames, our lives were in immediate danger.

My brother had been kept from screaming aloud by

my mother's firm pressure of her hands over his mouth, but he finally broke from her with the exclamation, 'I will go, for I had rather be killed by the Indians than to be burned to death.' He then struggled between the narrow passages by the palmetto posts, and passing down to the trap door, made a spring and lifting himself into the opening, jumped down into the water and made for the land. Our suspense was intense and we waited with baited breath for the rifle shot that would announce his death. When no sound was heard and we realized that for some time we had not seen a boat pass and we hoped that the Indians had gone.

We could no longer stay in our hiding place. We could not pass through the narrow space that my brother did, and with her hands my mother dug away the marl from the foot of one of the posts until she could drop it down and thus we passed through and under the burning wharf, and the coals fell upon us. When we reached the trap door, Mother helped me to reach to the top, then lifting my sick sister, I dragged her up and helped her down to the other side, then reached my hands down and thus helped Mother to get up. We then jumped down and taking my sister by her arm, Mother on one side and I on the other, we started for the land.

At that moment we espied at the side of the wharf a ship's launch moored. It was about 200 or 300 feet away. We also saw my brother standing in front of Houseman's store and his attention being attracted, we beckoned him to go down on the wharf and get into the boat, and we waded through the water which was then nearly up to our waist. About three miles from us there lay at anchor a schooner that had come loaded with canoes for the proposed expedition into the Everglades. We of course steered for this vessel. Mother had an Indian paddle, my brother a 'setting pole' and I an oar.

Small spots on the horizon warned the Indians that the wreckers from Key Tavernier and the three naval schooners were on their way to our relief. They set fire to the other houses and made all speed to Upper Matacumba. We drifted with the tide until the captain's boat overtook us, and as they drew near, for the first time, we began to realize our nearly naked condition. Sarah had on her nightgown, while mother and I having taken ours off on account of the warm night, had on but one garment. Henry was entirely naked, having taken his shirt off and tied it to a pole as a signal of distress to any passing vessel. Quickly Mother took a mosquito bar that was in the boat and tearing it in two wrapped its folds about us just as the captain and his two negro sailors caught hold of our boat and took us in their arms and carefully put us in their boat, the negroes begging us not to cry, saying, 'Oh, don't cry, missus; don't cry; you are safe now, missus; you are safe now.'

We soon reached the schooner's side and there found to our great delight that nearly all of the inhabitants had escaped. There had been 70 souls on the island, and of these there were but 13 missing. The Indians, by attacking the two larger houses first, had given the others a chance to get to their boats, and of course all had steered for this schooner.

Indian Key interior showing house and cistern foundations. All of the buildings on the island were burned by Seminoles in 1840 and only a few were rebuilt.

The escape for the island inhabitants was made easier on that fateful night and the next morning after the Indians found Housman's stash of liquor.

Around sunrise after the attack, while the Indians still occupied the island, two naval barges, each armed with a four-pound swivel gun, approached Indian Key intent on repelling the Indians. But the Seminoles effectively began using one of the island's six-pound cannons, and the naval assault was soon repelled. It was perhaps the first and only incidence of Seminoles using a captured cannon during the war.

The Seminoles burned and destroyed everything of value on Indian Key they could not carry away. They left that afternoon with thirty-four boats loaded with plunder. A naval commander later estimated that the warriors numbered about 134. The main motivation of the raid was believed to be the storehouse of goods on the island.

Dr. Perrine's remains were buried near a Sisal plant on Matecumbe Key, a plant that had once piqued his interest as something with which to develop a fiber industry. Jacob Housman, his town in ruins, sold what he could and returned to salvage work. He was killed shortly thereafter in heavy seas after being crushed between a wrecking vessel and a stricken ship. Chakaika, the Seminole leader, was killed a few months after the Indian Key raid when Colonel Harney led a surprise attack on his Everglades hammock. Chakaika was shot in the head trying to surrender and his body hanged. The bodies of two other male Seminole prisoners in his band were also hanged. The spot of the camp was later called "Hanging People" by the Seminoles.

The town of Indian Key was rebuilt by a couple of the original families and by the Florida Squadron, about six hundred men who were stationed there. After the war, the island's population swelled and receded at different times, and by the twentieth century, it was mostly inhabited by the occasional hermit, fisherman, or mariner. Eventually, the state of Florida purchased the island and it is now called the Indian Key Historic State Park, open during daylight hours.

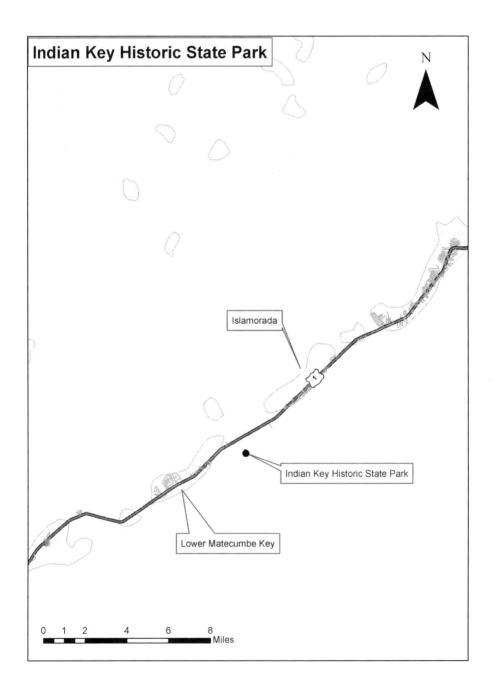

Indian Key Historic State Park

N

Islamorada

Indian Key Historic State Park

Lower Matecumbe Key

0 1 2   4   6   8
                              Miles

Indian Key street signs with original names of the streets in 1840.

Getting There

Today, visitors can take a tour boat to Indian Key—or take a private boat or kayak—and walk through the town's ruins on the original streets and climb an observation tower. Mostly foundations and cisterns carved from the coral rock can be seen, and most of the island has re-vegetated itself. Interpretive signs mark the house sites and the original streets have been cleared as paths.

Boats can land on the island's dock on the west side while there is a small sand landing for kayaks on the north side. Much of the island is surrounded by thick mangroves and sharp coral rock, deterring an easy landing, and one must wonder how the Seminoles managed at night with their seventeen canoes.

Boats and kayak rentals are available from Robbie's Marina at (305) 664-9814, Mile Marker 78.5 along U.S. 1. For more information about the park, call (305) 644-2540.

Eleven
Other Seminole War Sites

This guide has covered most of the major sites from the First and Second Seminole Wars that are open to the public, but there are numerous other sites along the Seminole Trail, some only marked by a sign or monument. Many more Second Seminole War sites are listed in this chapter in geographical order from north to south, and a Third Seminole War site is covered at the end.

The Museum of Florida History in Tallahassee

Numerous exhibits and cultural items relating to the Seminole Indians, including nineteenth-century lithographic prints of Seminole and Creek leaders, can be found at the museum in downtown Tallahassee, about two blocks west of the capitol building. Be sure not to miss the life-size bronze statues on the north side of the building that depict Native American life ranging from Calusa to Seminole Indians during different time periods. The museum is open Monday through Friday from 9 a.m. to 4:30 p.m., Saturdays from 10 a.m. to 4 p.m., and Sundays and holidays from noon to 4:30 p.m. Admission is free. The address is R.A. Gray Building, 500 South Bronough Street, Tallahassee, 32399-0250; (850) 245-6400. To learn more, log onto http://museumoffloridahistory.com/.

1830s Seminole warrior statue created by Brad Cooley outside of the Museum of Florida History in Tallahassee.

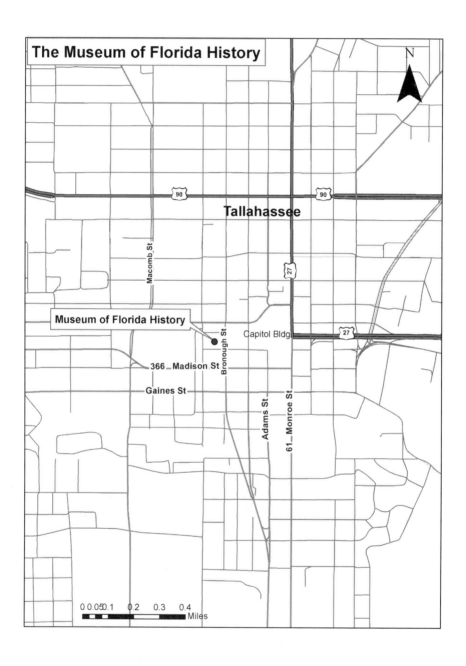

Fort Fanning along the Suwannee River

While the main body of Seminoles was being driven into south Florida, refugee Creek Indian bands were fleeing into Florida following the Creek War of 1836, trying to resist removal to Indian Territory. They sometimes joined remnant Seminole bands and began raiding homesteads.

Built in 1838 along a sweeping bluff of the Suwannee River, across from the site of Seminole and Black Seminole villages destroyed during the First Seminole War at Suwannee Old Town, Fort Fanning served to guard an important river crossing and to serve as a base of operations. By 1842, a main focus was on capturing the Creek war chief Octiarche and his followers, although this proved unsuccessful. At war's end, the fort was abandoned. In all, 31 soldiers lost their lives during the fort's occupation, mostly from disease. They were buried in a nearby military

Fort Fanning historic site in Fanning Springs along the Suwannee River.

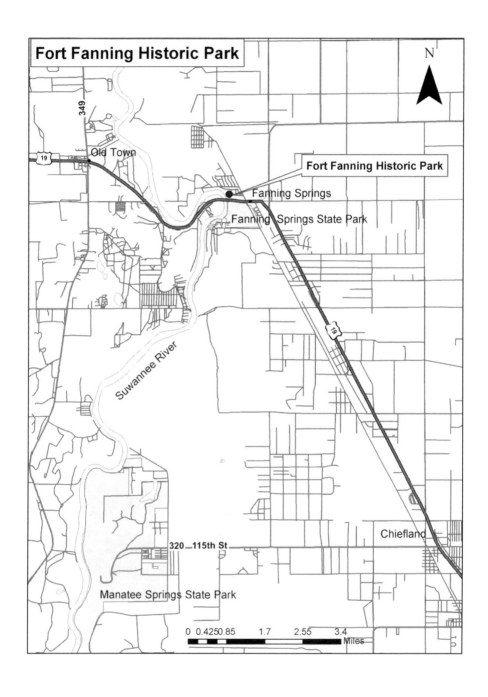

cemetery. The fort was named after Colonel Alexander Fanning, who served in both the First and Second Seminole Wars.

Fort Fanning Historic Park, in downtown Fanning Springs on the north side of the Highway 19 Bridge over the Suwannee River, commemorates the fort site with paved walkways and a reconstructed log gate. For more information, log onto http://www.exploresouthernhistory.com/fortfanning.html.

San Felasco Hammock near Gainesville

On September 18, 1836, this 7,360-acre preserve was the site of a skirmish during the Second Seminole War in which Colonel John Warren and the Florida militia engaged the Seminoles in an hour-and-a-half-long battle. The Seminoles eventually retreated due to heavy artillery fire. Losses on both sides were believed to be heavy, but no specific numbers are known. The San Felasco Hammock Preserve State Park is open during daylight hours seven days a week and features hiking, biking, and equestrian trails. Entrance for the hiking trail is at 11101 Millhopper Road, Gainesville, 32653, and the entrance for the other trails is at 13201 Progress Blvd., Alachua, 32615. For more information, log onto http://www.floridastateparks.org/sanfelascohammock/.

In 2011, a reenactment of the battle was held at nearby O'Leno State Park by the "Florida Frontier Guard" Seminole Wars Living History Association, 1835–1842. For more information about future reenactments, log onto http://www.floridafrontierguard.com/id17.html.

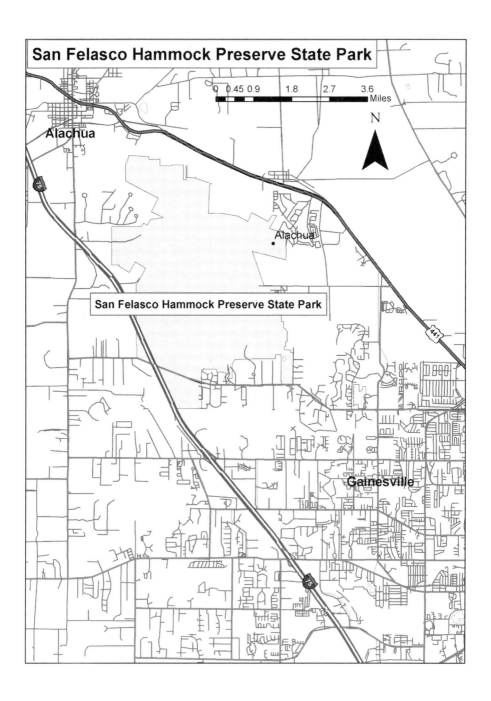

San Felasco Hammock Preserve State Park

Fort Cooper State Park near Floral City

In April 1836, when the Seminoles were still strong in number along the Cove of the Withlacoochee, Major Mark Anthony Cooper had the grim task of staying behind to protect the sick and wounded while General Winfield Scott continued on his way to Fort Brooke. Cooper was promised relief troops in nine days. Commanding 380 First Georgia Battalion Volunteers and a small artillery company, Cooper supervised the construction of a stockade on the western bluff of Lake Holathlikaha. On the third day, his position was discovered by Seminoles, who began to storm the fort daily. On one occasion, the Seminoles attacked with an estimated five hundred warriors. Instead of the promised nine days, the relief column returned in 16 days, but Cooper's leadership during the two-week siege resulted in only minimal losses. The fort continued to be used sporadically until 1842.

Fort Cooper State Park is open daily from 8 a.m. until sundown. Periodic living history programs and demonstrations are held, and the park also offers canoeing, hiking, and camping. A battle reenactment is held every April as part of Fort Cooper Days. The address is 3100 South Old Floral City Road, Inverness, FL 34450; (352) 726-0315; http://www.floridastateparks.org/fortcooper/default.cfm.

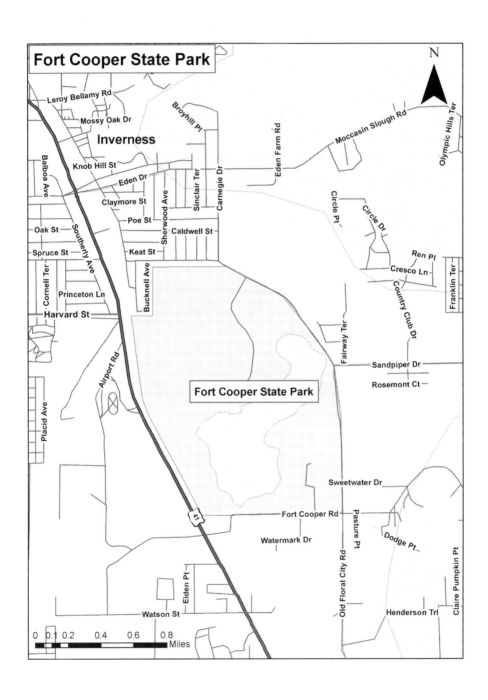

Fort Lane Park, Seminole County

In December 1837, General Jesup was pursuing retreating Seminoles into central and south Florida. To support his large army, Jesup established a chain of supply depots about thirty miles apart, roughly a day's march. Fort Lane was built as the first depot in the chain along the western shore of present-day Lake Harney. It operated only four months before being rendered obsolete since the theater of war had moved into south Florida.

The fort was named after Lieutenant Colonel John Foote Lane who had overseen a large Creek Indian regiment. He came down with "brain fever" (encephalitis) and committed suicide by sword in October 1836. The fort site is now a park owned and operated by the Geneva Historical and Genealogical Society. It is open seven days a week during daylight hours. The park can be accessed by driving east on Highway 46 from Sanford. After passing through Geneva and crossing the St. Johns River, turn north on Jungle Road. After a mile, turn right onto Fort Lane Road and follow to the park. For more information, log onto: http://www.usgennet.org/usa/fl/county/seminole/Geneva/fort_lane_park.htm.

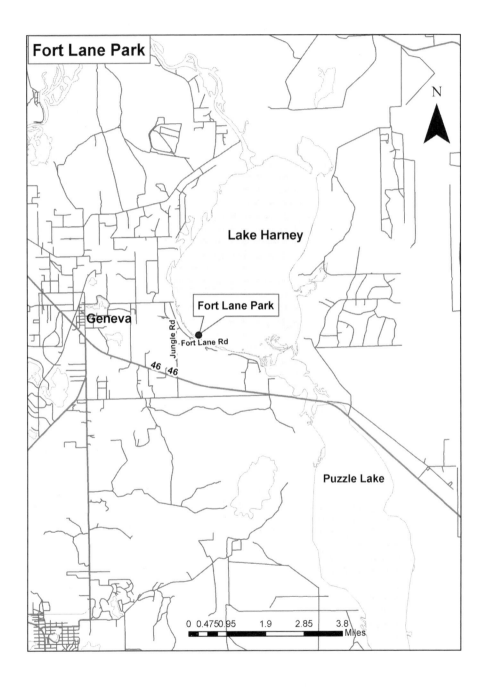

Fort Lane Park

Lake Harney

Fort Lane Park

Geneva

Jungle Rd

Fort Lane Rd

46 46

Puzzle Lake

N

0 0.4750.95   1.9   2.85   3.8
                                      Miles

Fort Christmas near Orlando

A full-size replica of Fort Christmas, complete with historical displays of Seminole culture and the Second Seminole War, greets visitors at Fort Christmas Historical Park just east of Orlando. Construction of the original fort was begun on Christmas Day in 1837 by 2,000 Army soldiers and Alabama Volunteers, thus the name. It was one of more than two hundred forts built during the war. The park also features seven restored pioneer homes. Various events are held throughout the year with Second Seminole War militia encampments set up on the weekend before Easter and the weekend before Thanksgiving. Hours for the fort and historic homes are Tuesday through Sunday from 9 a.m. to 4 p.m., while the overall park is open during daylight hours seven days a week.

The reconstructed Fort Christmas just east of Orlando.

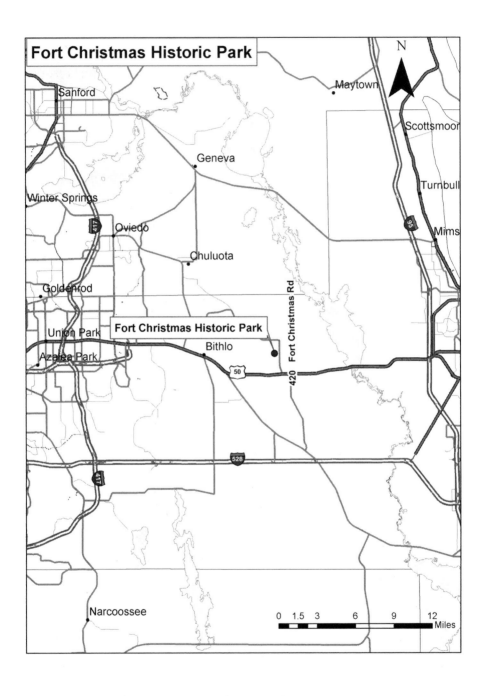

Fort Christmas Historic Park

Seminole display inside the reconstructed Fort Christmas.

Entrance is free. The address is 1300 Fort Christmas Road (C.R. 420), Christmas, 32709; (407) 254-9310. For more information, log onto http://www.nbbd.com/godo/FortChristmas/.

Loxahatchee River Battlefield Park

Southeast Florida's Loxahatchee River was the site of two Second Seminole War battles. The first battle, on January 15, 1838, was a clear victory for the Seminoles. Lieutenant Levin M. Powell was leading inexperienced Naval personnel who made up the United States Navy's Waterborne Everglades Expeditionary Unit when they encountered a larger body of Seminoles than they were equipped to handle. A massacre was only prevented by the rear guard action directed by Joseph E. Johnston.

The second Loxahatchee battle was a different matter. Just nine days after Powell's defeat, Major General Thomas S. Jesup marched 1,500 troops to the river where he was met by three hundred Seminoles along the river banks. He led a charge and was wounded, while the Tennessee Volunteers, commanded by Major William Lauderdale, took the brunt of the casualties. The Seminoles retreated into the swamps only when Colonel William Harney and his Dragoons pressured the Seminoles from their flank. Seven soldiers died and 31 were wounded in what would become the last standing battle of the Second Seminole War, giving way to more guerilla-type warfare.

Soon after the battle, Jesup promised the last free Seminoles they could remain in the south Florida interior. When his pledge was denied by Secretary of War Joel Poinsett in March, 1838, Jesup abruptly rounded up more than five hundred Seminoles under a white flag of truce at Fort Jupiter and shipped them to Indian Territory.

According to Seminole leader Betty Mae Jumper, in her autobiography, *A Seminole Legend*, her ancestors were camped on the Loxahatchee River thinking that the peace agreement was still in place. "One day when most of the men were out hunting, soldiers suddenly came and surrounded a camp of Seminoles, mostly old men, women, and children, along a river," she wrote. "That is why the river there was from that day

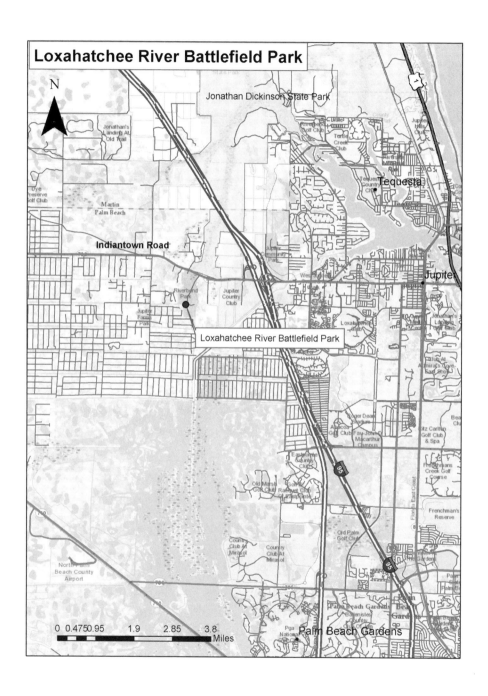

on called 'Lo-tsa-hatchee,' meaning 'River of Lies' in Creek, because our people thought that peace had been made. The soldiers gathered the Indians like criminals, making them all sit down in the open fields. Some were lucky enough to run away, and those who escaped ran to other camps to warn them." The name *Lo-tsa-hatchee* was later changed to Loxahatchee, River of Turtles.

Jesup left the Florida campaign having killed more than a hundred Seminoles and sending about 2,900 to Indian Territory, and he faced recriminations about his method of captures under truce flags for the rest of his life.

The 64-acre Loxahatchee River Battlefield Park, adjacent to Riverbend Park, is open seven days a week during daylight hours. The physical address to the park's entrance is 9060 Indiantown Road, Jupiter, 33478. It is conveniently located near I-95 and the Florida Turnpike about a mile west of the Indiantown Road (S.R. 706) exit to Jupiter. Periodic tours, living history programs, and historical reenactments are provided by the Loxahatchee Battlefield Preservationists. Black Seminoles gather each January at the park to commemorate the two battles and to honor their ancestors. For more information, log onto: http://loxahatcheebattlefield.com/.

Snake Warrior's Island Natural Area in Broward County

This site is one of the earliest Seminole settlements in the eastern Everglades, home of the Miccosukee leader Chitto Tustenuggee, or Snake Warrior. Historians speculate that it was occupied for more than a dozen years before the inhabitants were attacked by soldiers led by Wil-

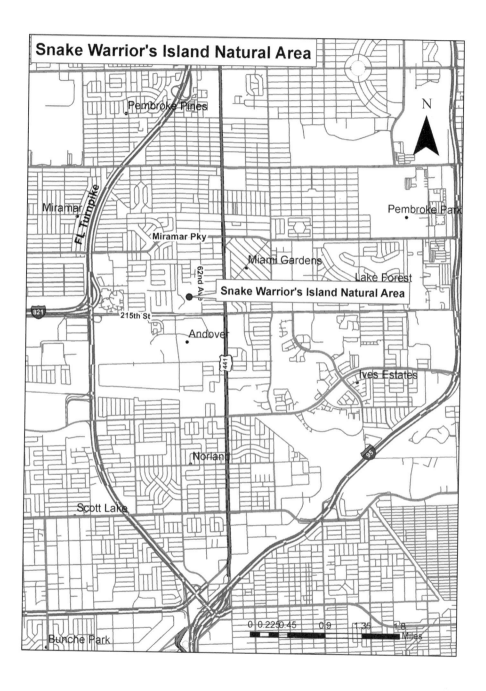

liam Harney and forced to flee in 1841. A soldier at the time reported that the area (once consisting of two islands before drainage) contained two towns, two dancing grounds and one council lodge, as well as a lush garden of pumpkin, squash, melon, lima bean plants, and even Cuban tobacco. Dance masks, kettles, baskets, and fish spears have also been found. Chitto Tustenuggee was designated by Seminole chief Arpeika, or Sam Jones, as his successor. However, he died in 1852, while Arpeika died after 1860 at the age of 100, although some accounts have him living even longer. By 1870, Seminoles again resettled the islands, led by Old Tiger Tail and Old Alec. They were forced to abandon the camps around the turn of the century due to encroaching development.

After the area was drained, the site was maintained as a pasture beginning in 1947, but the threat of development in 1992 prompted the 53-acre site to be purchased by the state of Florida through the Emergency Archaeological Property Acquisition Fund, with assistance from the Trust for Public Land and at the urging of the Seminole Tribe of Florida and Broward County. Broward County took control of the property in 2004 and manages it as a public natural area, open during daylight hours.

The Snake Warrior's Island Natural Area is located between S.W. 62nd Avenue and S.W. 64th Avenue south of S.W. 63rd Street in Miramar in Broward County. The address is 3600 S.W. 62nd Ave., Miramar, FL 33023; (954) 357-5161.

Cape Florida Lighthouse, Miami

As the Seminoles were being driven south into the Florida peninsula, south Florida settlements—including the lighthouse on Key Biscayne or Cape Florida—became more vulnerable to attack. Joan Gill

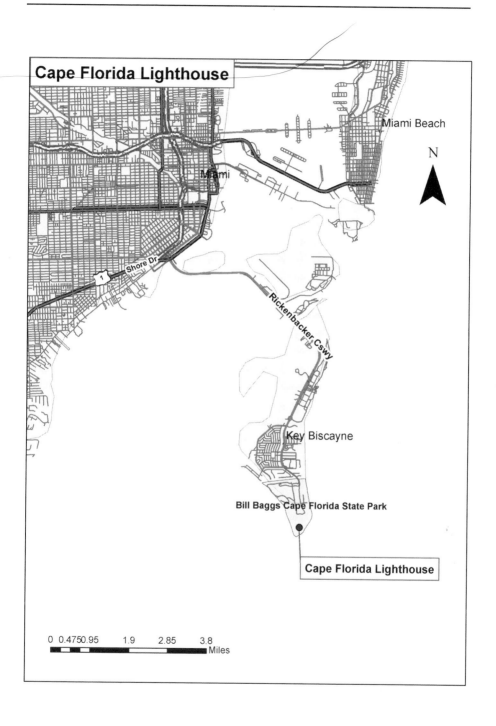

Cape Florida Lighthouse

Miami Beach

N

Miami

Shore Dr

1

Rickenbacker Cswy

Key Biscayne

Bill Baggs Cape Florida State Park

Cape Florida Lighthouse

0 0.4750.95   1.9   2.85   3.8
Miles

Blank, in her book *Key Biscayne,* describes what the lighthouse might have represented to the Seminoles: "From the Everglades and from the ridge, the Indians could see the lighthouse clearly, for vegetation was low and there were no obstacles to viewing. It must have seemed a disturbing silhouette against the sky by day; by night its light was unlike any star of the universe. It is likely that they came to loathe its unnatural incandescence, destroying the canopy of darkness, intruding into nature's spaces, and seeming to spy into their retreat."

Lighthouse keeper John Dubose warned of a possible attack, but his concerns fell on deaf ears. When Dubose sailed to Key West on leave in July 1836, and two other men were entrusted to the light, John W. Thompson and Aaron Carter, forty to fifty Seminole warriors arrived by canoes. Thompson and Carter took refuge in the tower, sawing away the stairs behind them, while bullets poured into the lighthouse windows and lanterns. The Seminoles burned the keeper's cottage and out buildings and began burning tins of oil around the tower. When heat became unbearable, the two keepers had to leave the lantern room and crawl onto the upper platform that circled the tower. Thompson was hit from several bullets in his feet and ankle while Carter was killed.

"The lamps and glasses bursting and flying all directions… and flesh roasting," Thompson reported. In desperation, he heaved a keg of gunpowder into the inferno and the resulting explosion alerted a ship several miles out to sea. The Seminoles soon left, but Thompson's ordeal was not over. Wounded and stuck atop the tower with no stairs, rescue attempts failed for more than a day until a line was fastened to the ramrod of a musket and shot over the tower, whereupon Thompson could grab hold and was soon rescued. Carter was buried beside the lighthouse. He is believed to be the only person ever to have been killed in defense of a lighthouse being attacked by Indians. A couple of years later, Fort Dallas was initially built around the hollowed lighthouse before being moved to the north bank of the Miami River. Before the lighthouse was rebuilt in 1846, the island served as a beacon for runaway slaves and Black Seminoles who gathered there before taking boats to the British Bahamas and freedom. The site has been designated a National Underground Railroad Network to Freedom Site.

The historic lighthouse on Key Biscayne can be visited at Bill Baggs Cape Florida State Park at 1200 South Crandon Boulevard, Key Biscayne, 33149; (305) 361-5811. The park is open during daylight hours 365 days a year. No camping is allowed except for organized youth groups. For more information, log onto http://www.florida stateparks.org/capeflorida/.

Miami's Fort Dallas

South Florida novelist Carl Hiaasen colorfully described Fort Dallas this way in his 1986 novel *Tourist Season:* "In the mid-1800s Miami was known as Fort Dallas. It was a mucky, rutted, steaming, snake-infested settlement of two hundred souls, perennially under attack from crafty Seminoles or decimated by epidemics of malaria. This was a time long before Fisher, Flagler, and the other land grabbers arrived to suck their fortunes out of North America's most famous swamp. It was a time when the local obsession was survival, not square footage, when the sun was not a commodity but a blistering curse."

Today, one can visit the old barracks of Fort Dallas in Miami's Lummus Park. The building was built from native oolitic limestone in 1844 and first used as a slave quarters on the William English plantation near the mouth of the Miami River. In 1843, William English was the first person to plat "the village of Miami." He went on to join the California Gold Rush, so when Fort Dallas was reestablished here in 1849 and 1855 to quell Seminole uprisings, the building served as a U.S.

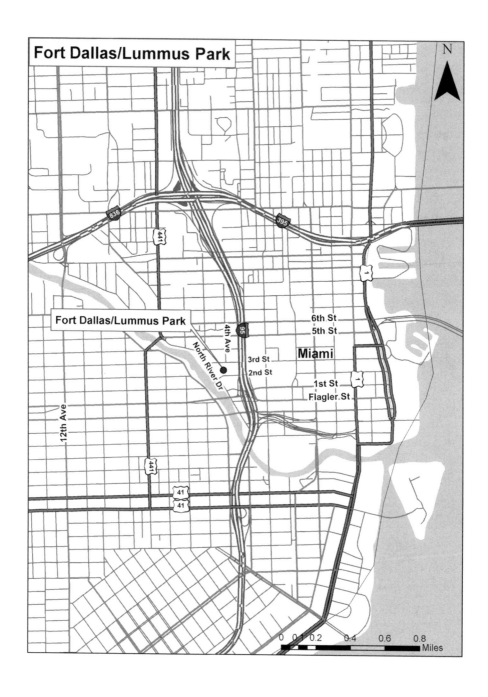

Army barracks. The fort was abandoned for the final time in 1858.

The building served various uses during the following decades but was slated for demolition in 1925 to make room for a high-rise hotel since Miami now represented a type of gold rush. The Miami Woman's Club and local chapter of the Daughters of the American Revolution succeeded in having the building disassembled and reconstructed in Lummus Park in Miami's downtown historic district. The barracks is the earliest surviving example of native limestone construction in Miami.

Lummus Park is adjacent to I-95 in downtown Miami. If heading south, exit at Flagler Avenue and the park is two blocks north. If heading north on I-95, exit at the Downtown Distributor (970) and head north three blocks on NW 2nd Avenue (968), then turn left on NW 3rd and travel one block. The address for Lummus Park is 404 N.W. 3rd Street, Miami, 33128; (305) 579-6935.

Paynes Creek Historic State Park along the Peace River

During a time when whites were encroaching on Seminole territory, thereby creating tensions between whites and Indians, authorities established a trading post along Paynes Creek near the Peace River in 1849. Renegade Indians attacked and destroyed the post that same year and killed the proprietors, Captain George Payne and Dempsey Whidden. This prompted the building of Fort Chokonikla nearby as the first in a chain of forts to control the Indians. The move proved to be successful, although the fort's occupants were said to have waged a losing battle against mosquitoes and associated plagues of malaria, and so the fort was closed the following year.

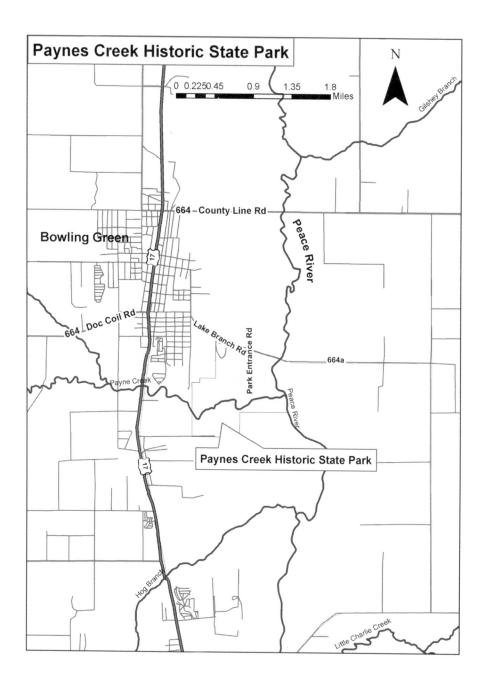

Today, visitors can walk the site of the early trading post and fort at Paynes Creek Historic State Park. A museum at the visitors center, open Thursday through Monday from 9 to 5, depicts Seminole Indians and early frontier life, and one can gain a better understanding of events that led to the Third Seminole War from 1855 to 1858. The address is 888 Lake Branch Road, Bowling Green, 33834; (863) 375-4717. To learn more, log onto http://www.floridastateparks.org/paynescreek/default.cfm.

Twelve
Emerging into the Twentieth Century

Smallwood Store and Stranahan House

*After the Seminole wars, Seminole holdouts began to come out of hiding to frequent south Florida trading posts. Two such trading posts survive as museums and are now stops along the Seminole Trail—the **Small-wood Store** in tiny Chokoloskee in the heart of the Ten Thousand Islands, and the **Stranahan House** in downtown Fort Lauderdale.*

"These Indians lead a quiet, peaceable, and semipastoral life, cultivating fields of corn, pumpkins, sweet potatoes, beans, bananas, etc., in the rich hamaks on the adjacent islands, their villages being in the pines on the border of the mainland [of the big island]. They also make starch from the "komptie," or wild arrowroot, which grows abundantly in the pine woods, and in the winter they hunt deer and bears. Such a life is not without its charms, shut out, as they are, from all the world by im-

penetrable cypress swamps, the only avenues to civilization being by way of the streams which drain the Everglades, the currents of which are so swift during high water that few attempt to ascend them to the Everglades, and still fewer succeed. In the spring and early summer the Everglades are comparatively dry; as Little Tiger said: 'In two moons, all water gone—canoe no go more.' During the autumn and winter the men go to the settlements, mostly to Miami on Biscayne Bay, by way of the Miami River, where they sell deerskins, buckskin, beeswax, komptie starch, vegetables, bird plumes, alligator teeth, etc., and buy cloth, calico, ammunition, tobacco, etc., and occasionally wy-ho-mee (whisky)."
—James A. Henshall, *Camping and Cruising in Florida,* 1884

After the Third Seminole War of the 1850s, one in which Billy Bowlegs and his band were forced to surrender and be relocated to Oklahoma, only around two hundred Seminoles remained in the Everglades region. Bands were scattered around the tree islands in the River of Grass, the thick swamps of the Big Cypress, along the rim of Lake Okeechobee, and north through the extensive Kissimmee River Valley, parts of which resemble the River of Grass. "These Indians withdrew from all willing contact with whites and existed for twenty years in isolation," wrote Brent Weisman in *Unconquered People.* "These two hundred were the cultural and biological Mayflower for the Seminoles and Miccosukees of today."

After living in seclusion for many years for fear of deportation, the remaining Seminole population in Florida gradually came out of hiding and began trading at general stores in and around the Everglades. Still, many were wary, as Minnie Moore-Willson wrote in 1896: "Visitors, traders and government agents have been denied their confidence, and it is only on their visits to settlements for the purpose of trading that they meet the white man. At such times the Seminole is on the alert, ever suspicious, and to the numerous interrogations applied to him by the inquisitive stranger, his answer is an indifferent 'Me don't know.' When questions become of a personal character, touching upon subjects sacred to a Seminole, he quietly walks away, leaving his questioner wondering."

Above Lake Okeechobee there were primarily Muscogee-speaking bands descended from upper Creeks. One band led by Chipco in the Lake Hamilton region was never located during the Third Seminole War. They eventually settled along Lake Pierce near the present-day Bok Tower. Chipco, who died in 1881, defied the stereotype of the suspicious Seminole and was famous for being friendly to whites. The band was taken over by his nephew, Tallahassee, who continued friendship with whites and even saved nearby families from starvation with gifts of deer and turkey. By the 1880s, they joined other bands along Cow Creek and Fisheating Creek, eventually becoming the Brighton Seminoles.

A commemorative plaque along Lake Hamilton in a small roadside park off U.S. 27 honors Chipco for his friendly relations with local settlers. It was dedicated in 1957 by the local chapter of the Daughters of the American Revolution.

Minnie Moore-Willson describes Chipco's heir, Chief Tallahassee, whom she met: "His countenance, while indeed mellowed with the cares of four-score years and ten, is kindly, and shows a conquered spirit. The lineaments of noble features are traceable in the broad forehead, the firm, thin lips, and eyes that might pierce the rays of the sun. Tallahassee shows no resentment to the white, yet he believes that they have treated the Indian badly. … Heaven forbid that any native of free America should wear so sad, almost heartbroken an expression as that which seams poor Tallahassee's face. No child could look upon it without being impressed by its mournful pathos. The very history of the tribe is carved there."

The high sandy ground of the Pine Island group of islands in the eastern Everglades became another refuge for Seminoles and Miccosukees during and after the Second and Third Seminole War. The region allowed for movement back and forth to the Shark River area in the heart of the Everglades River of Grass and to Biscayne Bay and the Keys. At least three major clan camps existed on Pine Island. Travel through the region was by foot when dry and by cypress canoes when water was high. Visitors in the 1880s commented on the comfort of the Pine Island chickee camps in pleasant natural surroundings.

Residents grew potatoes, bananas, corn, pumpkins, and lima beans in rich hammock soil. Nearby woods provided coontie roots. They traded bird plumes, hides, and furs at the Stranahan store in Fort Lauderdale and Brickell store on the Miami River for pots and pans, powder and bullets, glass beads and cloth. In later years, Ivy Stranahan recalled seeing "as many as a hundred canoes coming down the river, loaded with Indian families, their trade goods, cookware, and animals headed for a rendezvous at the trading post." Though the number of canoes may have been exaggerated since there were likely fewer than six hundred Seminoles at the turn of the century, Seminole groups came to the store as often as every six weeks if their supply of game was sufficient.

As chronicled in *The Stranahans of Fort Lauderdale* by Harry A. Kersey Jr., Ivy Stranahan began to educate many of the Indian children and eventually lobbied the government to set aside a reservation in Dania for the Seminoles. She helped to form the "Friends of the Seminoles" group, similar to Minnie Moore-Willson's "Friends of the Florida Seminoles" society but with a slightly different political focus. Stranahan's group helped to fund Seminole educational opportunities, among other things, including sending six Seminole young people to the Cherokee Indian School in North Carolina in 1937. One of those students was Betty Mae Tiger Jumper, who would later become the first woman elected as Seminole tribal leader. Jumper said of Stranahan, "She was the first person to buy me a dress so that I could go off to the Cherokee school. She helped me much of my life." Later, in her seventies, Stranahan lobbied to prevent termination of the tribe in the 1950s, believing they were not yet ready to manage their affairs without government assistance.

During the trading era of the early 1900s, on the opposite side of the Everglades from the Stranahan Store, George Storter operated a trading post in Everglades City. His nephew, Rob Storter, described the bustling store in *Crackers in the Glade:* "One summer over ten thousand alligator hides were shipped out to Tampa from my uncle's general store. He took in hides and furs from the Seminole Indians. I spent lots of time around at the store watching the Indians trade and measure their gator hides. Sometimes this would last all day." Seminole families would stay for several days at the store, and Storter wrote down observations of their life. In return for alligator hides, otter pelts, and bird plumes, the Seminoles received pots and pans, tools, guns and traps, coffee, tea, canned goods, clothes, hand-cranked sewing machines, and milled grits.

According to James Lafayette Glenn, who was appointed Special Commissioner to the Florida Seminoles in 1931, crimes among the Seminoles such as murder, theft, and adultery were "gotten rid of through execution" because evil powers were in their blood. This carried over to dealings with trading posts. "George Storter says that when a certain young Indian stole some of his merchandise, and he proved to the chief this fact, the chief brought him the offender and said, 'Here, you take him and kill him,'" Glenn wrote in *My Work among the Florida Seminoles.* Of course, Storter did no such thing. In reality, while murderers were often executed, other crimes were often forgiven at the annual Green Corn Ceremony.

Of the trading posts in the Everglades City area, only the Smallwood Store in nearby Chokoloskee still survives. When its doors were shut in 1982 and it ceased to be an active trading post, ninety percent of the original goods remained. The owner's granddaughter has since reopened it as a museum. Visitors can glimpse Everglades frontier life and learn about how the Seminoles lived and traded goods in the late 1800s and early 1900s. Paintings and historical displays offer a glimpse into the life of both early settlers and Seminoles who lived in the area. Illegal activities were commonplace and local hunters, including Seminoles, often killed wading birds for their plumes long after the practice was outlawed. Only a change in ladies' fashions put an end to the practice. By then, wading birds had been severely depleted.

Thelma Smallwood vividly recalls some encounters with the Seminole Indians at her father's trading post in the book *The Story of the Chokoloskee Bay Country* by Charlton W. Tebeau, first published in 1955:

> The Indians used to come in here and camp on the beach. At Christmas time there might be a hundred Indians. The men would all get drunk but one. He would bring their knives, guns, etc., in the store for my father to put under the counter until they got sober. When I was small some of the Indians would bring eight-pound lard buckets full of silver coins to my father to keep until they needed the money. They did not like paper money. One time my father gave an Indian a gold piece instead of a silver half dollar and he brought it back to my father in a few minutes. Father didn't know what was wrong until he looked at the money...
>
> They also came in for medicine when they were sick. He knew their language and customs and they trusted him. In the 1918 epidemic, influenza spread to the Indians at the head of Turner River. Many of them were dying with it. Their medical lore provided no remedy for this new disease. They were said to pour cold water on the feverish ones to cool them.

According to Thelma Smallwood, her father's accounting books from 1914 showed that he was buying or trading for alligator hides from

Smallwood Store Museum in Chokoloskee, Ten Thousand Islands.

Miami Billy, Little Jim Dixie, Little Charlie Jumper, Little Boy Jim, Jim Tiger, Charlie Billy, Charlie Doctor, and Jack Osceola. Seven-foot hides brought ninety cents to a dollar apiece. The Indians also supplied islanders with fresh venison and turkey and sometimes wild berries. In turn, the Seminoles received hand-crank sewing machines, sewing thread and needles, yards of calico, phonographs and records, accordions, sugar, flour, and coarse grits.

In order to obtain goods for survival and for commerce and trading, hunting and fishing remained a big part of Seminole life.

The late Mary Frances Johns, a traditional Seminole elder who lived on the Brighton Reservation along Lake Okeechobee, recalled in 2000:

Growing up on the Tamiami Trail, we lived at a place called Royal Palm Hammock where we had both fresh and briny water. This gave us access to many types of fish. We either gigged the fish with a single or five-prong spear, or used a fishing pole. Sometimes, we'd even wade in shallow water and chop their heads off with a machete. It was more fun to gig them.

One time when I was about five or so, ignoring my grandmother's warning never to gig a big fish, I gigged this snook that was twice as big as I was. Well, as you might imagine, five year old scrawny me hung onto the bridge railing screaming for all my worth for Grandma to come and rescue me. The harder the fish fought, the more determined I was to hang onto the fish. It never once occurred to me that all I had to do was to release the loop of string around my wrist. Boy oh boy, was Grandma ever mad at me! For days she would not let me near the water, but we did eat well for a couple of days.

Many visitors and residents were impressed by the character of the Seminoles they encountered during the trading post days. One traveler was Hugh L. Willoughby, who paddled across the Everglades in a canoe in 1897: "The occasional visits which he [a Seminole] makes to the trading-stations do him no good, as there he finds the 'white man's fire-water,' which he is tempted to imbibe too freely by those who think themselves of a superior race, but who, in reality, are far inferior to the 'untutored Indian' in every moral trait. ... A Seminole would as soon cut his tongue out as lie." Willoughby mentioned that the Seminoles were friendly to whites during the period of his contact with them, but secretive as to Everglades travel and geography. "They may take you out, but never in," he concluded.

Completion of the Tamiami Trail in 1928 marked the end of Seminole trading at the Smallwood Store. The road cut across several long-standing canoe trails, impeding travel. Plus, Seminoles could now drive to larger markets and stores in vehicles rather than paddle canoes, and the road opened up more hunting areas to non-Indians, further reducing game populations and thus, Indian trade items. The Seminole way of life began to change again.

One way to experience travel in the Ten Thousand Islands around the Smallwood Store is to canoe or kayak the backwaters, or to go by motorboat or guided tour. There aren't ten thousand islands—more like two hundred—but the maze of tidal creeks and mangrove islands is impressive. One needs good maps and a GPS system and compass to keep from becoming lost—unless, of course, you have a Seminole guide or other area resident who knows the waters. Several of the islands are good spots to camp with permits from Everglades National Park, and fishing is still popular and can yield good results.

Also in the area is the Collier-Seminole State Park along the Tamiami Trail (U.S. 41) just west of the road to Everglades City and Chokoloskee. The park was established as a memorial to the Seminole wars, and the park's visitor center is patterned after a blockhouse from that era. The park also honors the wealthy entrepreneur Barron Collier, who helped finance both the park and the building of the Tamiami Trail. As mentioned, the road changed the lives of Seminoles and Miccosukees living in the region, and the park houses the Bay City Walking Dredge that was used to build the roadbed through the vast wetlands. At 7,271 acres and protecting one of three original stands of royal palms in Florida, Collier-Seminole State Park is as much a monument to the natural environment as it is to the historical people who have shaped the landscape. Visitors can bike on a 3.5-mile historic road, hike a 6-mile portion of the Florida National Scenic Trail, or paddle a 13.5-mile loop trail through a mangrove-dominated wilderness.

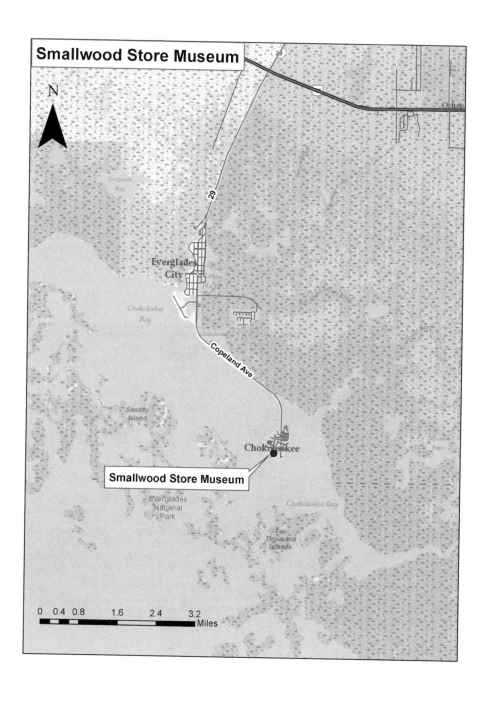

Getting There

S mallwood Store is located in the tiny town of Chokoloskee in the Ten Thousand Islands.

Collier-Seminole State Park is located 15 miles east of Naples along the Tamiami Trail (U.S. 41) and CR 92 and is open during daylight hours. Camping and cabins are also available in the park. The address is 20200 E. Tamiami Trail, Naples, Florida 34114; (239) 394-3397.

Stranahan House, built in 1901 by Frank and Ivy Stranahan and having once served as a trading post for Seminoles as well as a post office, community center, restaurant, and home to the Stranahans, is now

A look inside the historic Smallwood Store in the Ten Thousand Islands. The store was once a major trading post for Seminole Indians.

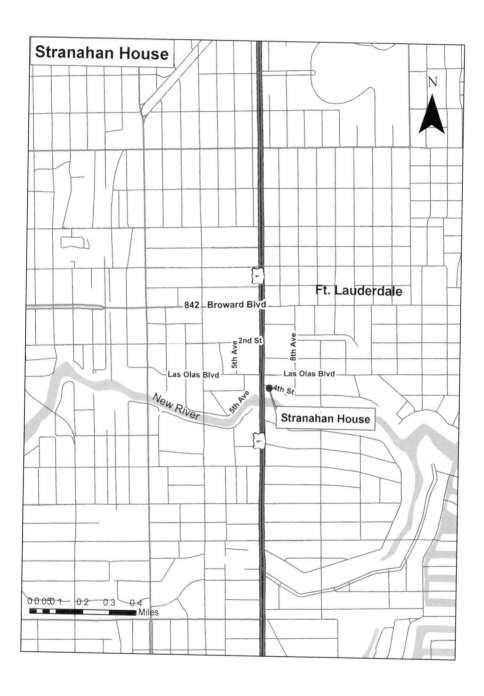

a museum. It stands on the original location along the New River in downtown Ft. Lauderdale. The eastern anchor of the River Walk linear waterfront park, it's open every day for tours at 1, 2 and 3 p.m. The museum is closed to the public in September. The address is 335 Southeast 6th Avenue, Fort Lauderdale, FL 33301; (954) 524-4736; info@stranahanhouse.org; http://stranahanhouse.org/.

Thirteen
The Rise of Tourism

Seminole and Miccosukee Villages

As the Everglades environment started shrinking due to development and drainage, the traditional Seminole hunting and fishing way of life began to suffer. A new venue emerged for the Seminoles—tourism. The Seminole Trail features two tourist villages still open to the public—the **Okalee Indian Village** *in Hollywood and the* **Miccosukee Indian Village** *along the Tamiami Trail, both of which feature the ever-popular alligator wrestling.*

When the East Coast Railway chugged into Miami for the first time in 1896, more intercultural contacts occurred between whites and Seminoles, and curious tourists wanted to visit Seminole camps. Seminole women took a more active economic role, selling hand-made items

M-144—Seminole Indian Boy and Parrot at Musa Isle Indian Village Miami, Florida

Early postcard of a Seminole boy with parrot at the Musa Isle Indian Village in Miami. (Florida Archives)

such as baskets, moccasins, and braided belts. Eventually, the Musa Isle Indian village was created as a major tourist attraction near Miami, followed closely by several others, including Coppinger's Tropical Gardens, Osceola's Gardens, Osceola's Indian Village, Tropical Hobbyland, and Alligator Joe's. Most families received six dollars a week plus food and tips at the camps.

Taking a photo of a camp Indian generally required a tip, and some Seminoles turned their backs on the photographer if the tip wasn't given. Other tourist photographic eye candy came in the form of Seminole wedding reenactments. Some young Seminole couples were married "traditionally" several times for the benefit of visitors, even though most traditional weddings were finalized at the privately held annual Green Corn Ceremony.

Soon after the camps were formed, alligators began to feature prominently in the attractions. While Seminoles were certainly accustomed to the ways of the alligator, having hunted them for many years and even capturing them and bringing them back to their villages so the meat would stay fresh, the first alligator "wrestler" in the Miami area was a white man who called himself Alligator Joe. Henry Coppinger Jr., owner of a Seminole tourist village near Miami, soon learned the trade and taught it to several Seminole men. Immediately, Seminole alligator wrestling got top billing because, to tourists, the activity seemed "authentic." It was easy to picture Seminole men, and perhaps some women, amusing themselves in the remote Everglades by wrestling with large saurians.

For a typical performance, an alligator wrestler would usually pull out a large alligator from a pit and do various maneuvers including climbing on its back, opening its jaws to show visitors its many teeth, and sometimes placing his head inside the mouth. Then, the wrestler would close its mouth and hold its jaw shut with his chin. Eventually, the alligator would be flipped over and its stomach rubbed until it passed out.

A few outsiders and at least one government Indian agent viewed the tourist villages, especially alligator wrestling, as degrading to the Seminoles. "These places point the road to stagnation and death," concluded Special Agent Roy Nash in a report to the United States Senate in 1931. "Earning one's living in competition with rattlesnakes and alligators leads nowhere." Nash urged that a law be adopted by the Florida Legislature making it unlawful to harbor Indians "for amusement purposes," a proposal that failed to gain traction due to the economic advantages of the villages to local towns and merchants.

Many Seminole alligator wrestlers took pride in the craft and modified and developed new moves. It was also lucrative. One wrestling episode to a large appreciate audience could net the wrestler a week's worth of wages in tips. The activity had its hazards, however, and that was part of the attraction. More than one wrestler lost digits or was otherwise injured, and at least two received head wounds from placing their heads into an alligator's mouth and failing to hold the mouth open long enough. Once an alligator clamped down on a head or limb, it often had to be shot and the jaw pried open with a crowbar!

Seminole tribal chairman James Billie—who began wrestling alligators at age five—famously lost a finger during an exhibition at the Billie Swamp Safari on the Big Cypress Reservation in 2000. Billie ordered that the alligator be kept alive. "The gator did his job. He won again," he said afterwards. "I want to honor that gator. With all the help they have given me, I guess (giving up a finger) is a small little payment . . . reminding me they can still dominate. Go gators!" It wasn't the first time Billie had been bitten. In 1977, his left thumb was almost severed, and in 1983, he was bitten in the buttocks while performing an alligator exhibition for actress Connie Stevens. In that incident, the bite came perilously close to his privates. "My voice changed," he joked.

Alligator wrestling generally belonged to the men's domain, but the late Seminole leader Betty Mae Jumper sometimes filled in for her husband at Al Starts's "Jungle Queen" Landing near Fort Lauderdale. Her husband, Moses, would sometimes fall into bouts of drinking to escape memories of Pacific fighting in World War II. "Sometimes, when he was too drunk to wrestle, I would get into the alligator pit myself," she wrote

Alligator wrestler Carlos Cabrera shows a classic Seminole wrestling move at the Miccosukee Indian Village off the Tamiami Trail.

in her autobiography, *A Seminole Legend.* "I did that because I needed to earn money to feed the kids. I wore my regular clothes, my Seminole skirt and blouse. The women tourists got really excited. 'Look! She's going to wrestle it!'" Betty Mae Jumper, once scorned as a half blood, went on to become the first chairwoman of the Seminole Tribe of Florida, serving from 1967 to 1971.

Besides alligator wrestling, other new activities emerged at the Indian villages such as totem pole carving. This custom was adapted from West Coast Native Americans and was deemed authentic, and after the first Seminole totem pole was carved in 1928, colorful totem poles soon decorated most of the villages. The list of souvenirs began expanding to include dolls, jackets, skirts, and beadwork. By 1930, more than half of all Florida Seminoles and Miccosukees were involved with tourism-related employment and nearly all of the remaining Indians were supplying goods for the tourist market.

In 1931, famed ethnomusicologist Frances Densmore, who recorded Seminole songs, marveled that the Florida Seminoles "have developed a commercial ability which makes them self-supporting, and they have succeeded in doing this with a minimum use of the English language."

The economic opportunities provided by the Indian villages came at the right time. The Seminole lifestyle was changing due to environmental degradation of the Everglades. Enormous draglines had moved in, draining the lifeblood that kept the vast wetlands alive. "In the old times we could paddle our canoes for many days and hunt the deer and the alligator," elder Pete Tiger said in 1956. "Now, the white man has drained the Glades with his canals to make fields for his tomatoes and sugarcane. Our canoes cannot run on the sand and it is forbidden to cross the white man's fences. And the deer and the alligator each day go farther away."

Seminole sympathizer Minnie Moore-Willson, a white woman from Kissimmee, tried to alert the country to the destruction in her second and third editions of *Seminoles of Florida*, published in 1910 and 1911 respectively. "To-day in the forest home of the Seminoles, where yet gleams the council fires, and within a mile of the palmetto thatched camp of the Osceola's, the big dredges groan an accompaniment, as it were, to the echo of the throbbing hearts, the death song, the Recessional, of the Seminole.

"Dynamite blasts shake the very pans and kettles hanging around the wigwams and, while this monster of a machine destroys the only home of the tribe, is the time not ripe for decisive action in the protection of these wards of Florida?"

Seminole elder Sam Huff was interviewed in 1952, and he summarized the destruction this way: "Steam shovels began to make canals in the Everglades. Steam shovels came out of Ft. Lauderdale, and others came out of Deerfield, heading for [Lake] Okeechobee. 'Just as soon as they hit the lake, the water is going to dry up in those Everglades, and as soon as the water dries up, they're going to start plantations'—that's what the white people said to the Indians. Another steam shovel went out from Dania, and another one from Miami. Just as soon as they hit Okeechobee, the water was going to dry up. But I didn't believe it, until they hit Okeechobee. Then the water dried up, and even in Okeechobee it was dry, too. The Everglades became small, and the trees grew very fast."

To add to the damage created by the canals and drainage, a road was built across the Everglades—the Tamiami Trail. Completed in 1928, the road opened up traditional Miccosukee country to tourists. The Miccosukees were often deemed Seminoles by the government and most outsiders, but they spoke a language descended from the lower Creek Indians while many Seminoles along the upper edge of Lake Okeechobee spoke Muscogee, the language of the upper Creeks. The Miccosukees—also called the Miccosukee Seminoles or the Miccosukee-speaking Seminoles—desired to be a separate entity for political reasons as well. In the 1920s and 1930s, more acculturated Seminoles and Miccosukees began moving to government reservations. They took up cattle grazing, sent their children to schools, and began working for the Bureau of Indian Affairs. About three hundred Miccosukees, however, remained sequestered in Everglades camps, following more traditional ways. They still traded for modern goods, but they retained their language and cultural ways.

After the Tamiami Trail was completed, several Miccosukee families moved from isolated camps to the new highway in order to take advantage of the tourist trade. Since they owned their camps, many families no longer traveled for stints at the white-owned villages near Miami, allowing for greater economic independence.

By 1939, Ethel Cutler Freeman observed that there were thirteen Indian camps along the trail that charged admission to tourists and sold souvenirs. "Although the Indians have left their homes in the wilds to gain a living from tourists, these camps along the Trail are not commercialized as one would expect," she wrote. "They live their lives independent of the white man who comes to look at them. In this way they are comparable with the owners of the old houses of Virginia and England who open their homes and gardens for gain—yet they are not seen and their lives are untouched and unaffected by their visitors to whom they are supremely indifferent."

Politically, the Seminole Tribe of Florida sought tribal recognition in the 1950s and it was granted in 1957. The Miccosukees, in turn, sought independent recognition but were snubbed by state and federal officials because, in the minds of many, they were merely a faction of the Seminoles. Undaunted, tribal leader Buffalo Tiger and other Miccosukee officials visited Cuba in 1959 soon after Fidel Castro took power. They were formally recognized as an independent nation by the Cuban government. This got the desired attention from United States government officials and the tribe became federally recognized in 1962. One unwritten caveat was that the Miccosukees spurn further contact with the Cuban government.

Cooking chickee at the Miccosukee Indian Village off the Tamiami Trail.

A third group of south Florida Indians, the Independent Traditional Seminole Nation, refused to join either tribe, choosing instead to live as traditionally as possible. When their ceremonial grounds were destroyed by a farming operation early in the twenty-first century, the Indian Law Resource Center, with the generous support of the Lannan Foundation, purchased 2,500 acres of undeveloped land for the group. Because the group follows traditional spiritual laws that forbid the ownership of land, the land is kept in trust on their behalf.

Today, thanks to Indian gaming and other enterprises, the Seminole Tribe of Florida does not need to rely on tourist villages. Still, the tribe maintains the Seminole Okalee Indian Village on their Hollywood Reservation, first opened in 1959, closed for a spell, and was renovated and reopened in 1998. Traditional arts and crafts, demonstrators, histori-

Minnie Lou Billie sews original patchwork clothing at the Miccosukee Indian Village off the Tamiami Trail.

cal displays, and a gift shop are all featured. Alligator wrestling is still a mainstay, although most wrestlers today are hired from outside the tribe. "WANTED: Alligator wrestlers," began a Seminole tribal ad in the *South Florida Sun Sentinel* in 2000. "Must be brave and a risk taker. Males and females o.k. No experience needed." Gaming has allowed young Seminole men the financial freedom to pursue more professional careers, such as business, communications, and law.

The Miccosukee Tribe still maintains tourist villages and camps along the Tamiami Trail, such as the Miccosukee Indian Village. The village features Miccosukee Indians engaged in the art of woodwork, beadwork, patchwork, doll making, and basket weaving, although one might find only one or two demonstrators on any given day with the exception of special events. Tribal paintings and historical artifacts are also displayed at the tribal museum as part of the village.

Alligator wrestling is a popular attraction at the Miccosukee Indian Village and several shows are performed daily, but like the Seminole Tribe of Florida, the Miccosukees began to hire from outside the tribe. Carlos Cabrera, a Hispanic, jumped at the opportunity to wrestle alligators at the Miccosukee Indian Village in 2005. "I love my job," he said in a 2012 interview with the author. "I have fun every single show." Before wrestling alligators five times a day, he constructed chickees at the village. He has been bitten on the hand, a puncture wound that required a trip to the hospital—"but I first finished the show," he said proudly.

Cabrera added, fingering a specially made crocodile tooth necklace, "I have great respect for the gators, but I'm not afraid of them. People think we are hurting the alligators, but we're not. They're not getting hurt in any way." That doesn't mean that the show alligators don't become agitated, and Cabrera frequently puts his hand in an alligator's mouth and quickly pulls it away as the gator snaps its jaw shut. These are not docile creatures.

At a 2012 show, Cabrera performed all of the classic alligator wrestling moves except putting his head in the alligator's mouth. Instead, he put his nose to the alligator's snout in an "Eskimo kiss."

In the book *Seminole Voices,* Jeannette Cypress said that Indian villages over the past century enabled Seminoles and Miccosukees to proudly show whites their history and culture. "I remember going, as a youngster, to this village in Miami. My parents had to go there and sew and do things in front of tourists. I did not think of it as being bad. And then I worked at a village… I was like a tour guide. I always felt like I was out there promoting the tribe in a positive way. I did not want people to stereotype us, like, oh, drunk Indians. You know, you hear that all the time. So, I guess it was a way for me to tell people. I had kids asking me, can you see in the dark? Where are your feathers? It was one way to tell them who we really were. I never thought anything bad [about it]."

Chickee and boardwalk at the Miccosukee Indian Village off the Tamiami Trail.

Mary Frances Johns stated that making and selling crafts—even if it was no longer an economic necessity—was a way to "publicize your people."

Despite the fact that gaming is the major economic engine for the Seminole and Miccosukee tribes, historian Patsy West in her 2008 study of contemporary Seminole history, *The Enduring Seminoles: From Alligator Wrestling to Casino Gaming*, maintains that these two tribes are eager to continue their tourist economy. In fact, according to West, "Tribal commitments to cultural and 'eco' tourism will play a major role in keeping these Native Americans in touch with their native environment and heritage, while their gaming proceeds will fund projects that those early pioneers of the Miami tourist attractions would never have thought possible. As other tribes gear up to reap tourist dollars on their reservations, the Florida Seminoles and Miccosukees are way ahead of the game."

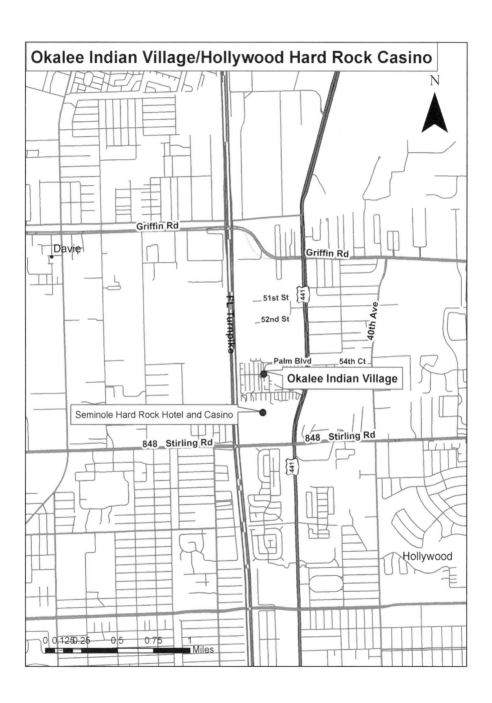

Getting There

The Okalee Indian Village is open Wednesday through Friday from 9:30 a.m. to 4:30 p.m., Saturdays from 12 p.m. to 9 p.m., and Sundays from 10:30 a.m. to 6:30 p.m. It is located just off State Road 7 (U.S. Highway 441) north of Stirling Road in Hollywood on the north side of the Hollywood Hard Rock Casino. The address is 5716 Seminole Way, Hollywood, 33314; (800) 683-7800. While on the Hollywood Reservation, you can also see the Council Oak near the corner of U.S. 441 and Stirling Road. The oak was a Seminole meeting spot for many years.

The Miccosukee Indian Village is open daily from 9 a.m. to 5 p.m. and is located along the Tamiami Trail about 30 miles west of Miami. Annual tribal-sponsored arts and music festivals at the village benefit the Miccosukee Educational Fund. The address is Mile Marker 70, U.S. Hwy. 41, Miami, FL, 33194; (305) 552-8365.

Early Seminole scene in the Miccosukee Museum, part of the Miccosukee Indian Village off the Tamiami Trail.

Fourteen
Everglades Home

The Everglades and Big Cypress Swamp continue to be home for Seminole and Miccosukee Indians. In this chapter, the Seminole Trail takes us through these unique environments and we see how the native inhabitants learned to adapt and survive.

While many soldiers and settlers saw the Everglades and the adjoining Big Cypress Swamp as a hellhole to avoid, the Seminoles realized it could support life, and hide them. This is where most of the Indians who eluded capture remained and never surrendered. A new home. It is, in most regards, the end of the Florida's Seminole Trail, but there is a fork here. The other branch goes to Indian Territory—Oklahoma—where the displaced Florida Seminoles had been moved. Eventually, the Oklahoma Seminoles developed a viable tribe of several thousand, while groups of Black Seminoles moved even farther west to Texas and Mexico, where many served with distinction as scouts for the

Alligators along Shark Valley Road in Everglades National Park.

United States Army. There is also a contingent of Black Seminoles who fled to the Bahamas on Andros Island, where they continue to identify themselves as such.

But Florida's Everglades, what the Seminoles called *Pa-Hay-Okee*— "grassy water"—is a common bond for many Seminoles. Whether you have zoomed across the open marshlands in an airboat, paddled a quiet dugout or modern canoe, hiked or waded through Big Cypress Preserve on the Florida National Scenic Trail, or sat on observation platforms in Everglades National Park as sunlight fades, you'll quickly realize the uniqueness and vastness of this wetlands.

White egrets, continually probing for food, stand out like luminaries with angular forms. More camouflaged red-shouldered hawks perch on dwarf cypress trees. The trees are only five feet tall, yet even these are

176

high enough for raptors to scan a wide area. Perches for living statues.

Unseen are loud bullfrogs and the occasional bellowing alligator. And somewhere, it is easy to imagine the scream of a Florida panther, and the voices and song of native peoples. Perhaps they are praying, man and beast, for the Everglades to survive.

What was once a completely natural system of lakes, wetlands, connecting streams, and rivers that flowed into the River of Grass is now controlled by pumps, canals, locks, and dams. Restoration and Everglades survival are in the form of complex and expensive plans that attempt to restore more sheet flow and water deliveries at traditional times of year, but they must also be balanced between the needs of agriculture and millions of people who now live to the east and west along the coasts.

Some of the native people who live in the sawgrass, the Seminole and Miccosukee, say it is their traditional songs and dances that have kept the Glades alive, and their lawsuits that have forced government agencies to clean up the water haven't hurt either.

Marjory Stoneman Douglas, author of *Everglades: River of Grass,* once likened Everglades restoration to a type of test. "If we pass," she said, "we may get to keep the planet."

What keeps the vision of an intact Everglades alive? Maybe because one can slosh or canoe through its waters and gaze out over its expanses and still feel the pulse of life. There are alligators, wading birds, and Everglades kites—not as many—but they are visible. Marsh rabbits, apple snails, water snakes, and garfish are more numerous, and somewhere in the vastness roams the Florida panther, highly endangered but slowly rising in numbers.

If you gaze across the Glades long enough, you might realize that despite our most ill-conceived plans and even our best intentions, the Everglades will survive. You can venture into the River of Grass with a soul yearning for wilderness, and find it—and realize why some Seminoles decided to stay in the 1830s, and remain today.

Born in a small village deep in the Everglades in 1920, Buffalo Tiger grew up as a traditional Miccosukee Seminole boy with no electricity and few modern conveniences, and without the requirement to attend school. His teachers were his elders; his classroom was the Everglades. In his autobiography, *Buffalo Tiger: A Life in the Everglades,* Buffalo Tiger described his early youth, one filled with hunting and fishing, growing edible plants and collecting wild ones, finding the right materials for building chickees, poling dugout canoes, understanding the natural elements, listening to talking animal stories in the evenings, and learning his people's customs and spiritual ways and how to carry oneself proudly and with respect for elders and all life.

"When you are little, being a Miccosukee, you have a clear mind, a

Airboat at Buffalo Tiger's Florida Everglades Airboat Rides takes visitors through the Everglades near the Tamiami Trail.

very clear mind about what you are," he wrote. "We had no idea about another life, the city life; we just learned and knew ourselves. We were so comfortable with our father and our grandmothers and our people and what they taught us. . . . We had no boundaries in this land, no fences. We were always free."

Not surprisingly, Buffalo Tiger and other traditionally raised Miccosukees and Seminoles developed a strong conservation ethic. They certainly took things from the environment—they hunted, fished, trapped, gathered wild foods, and cut trees, but they sought to take only what they needed. "Traditional Indians held deep feelings about the land in part because their life depended on it," he concluded. "Our ancestors taught us to remember we are part of this earth and we must protect it. We must not destroy or sell it." He cautioned that many modern Miccosukees have lost that connection with the land. "Land is more important than money. ... Our grandfathers and their grandfathers loved this earth. Because of their feelings for the land, we live here today."

Life wasn't always easy in the Everglades. There could be hordes of mosquitoes and other flying insects, against which smoky fires, smudge pots, various animal and fish oils, and wild herbs were only partially effective. Then, there were hurricanes. Buffalo Tiger was a young boy hunting with a family group when the big hurricane of 1926 began to sweep through. His family sought the highest hammock they could find. When it became obvious that the worst was about to hit, they found an old, sturdy-looking tree, one that had withstood many hurricanes, and tied a canvas around it. Then, they put the children inside, including Buffalo Tiger.

"We survived because us kids moved together, and we used all kinds of blankets to keep ourselves warm," he wrote. "Even though our faces were cold, our bodies were warm." The children also passed around a warm baby, their little brother, to help keep warm. When they returned to their camps, most of the chickees were under water, everything blown down or washed away, and it was difficult to find food, but they had survived.

In the 1970s, the Miccosukees became the first tribe to take complete control of their affairs and federal budget, starting a national trend for Native American tribes. The tribe also filed lawsuits to help clean up water flowing through the Everglades and to maintain a more natural flow cycle. "As for Everglades' water, everything has changed," said former tribal chairman Buffalo Tiger. "The water was very clean years ago. Miccosukees would swim in the Glades water and drink it. Today people are saying that the water is not clean. You can tell that is true because it is yellow-looking and does not look like water you would want to drink. You probably get sick from drinking it. That means that fish or alligators in the water are not healthy; white men did that, not Indians. Miccosukees were told that was what was going to happen many years ago, and now it has. We cannot just say that the water is no good or the land is no good and turn our back on that."

Bikers and hikers along Shark Valley Road in Everglades National Park.

The late Mary Johns added in a 2000 interview, "Fish conservation is a concern to us now because the Everglades has been drained of the usual amount of water it takes to breed fish in abundance," she said. "These people who made decisions to make more arable and more habitable land did not stop to consider the value of these wetlands to our food supply!"

Great blue heron along
Shark Valley Slough.

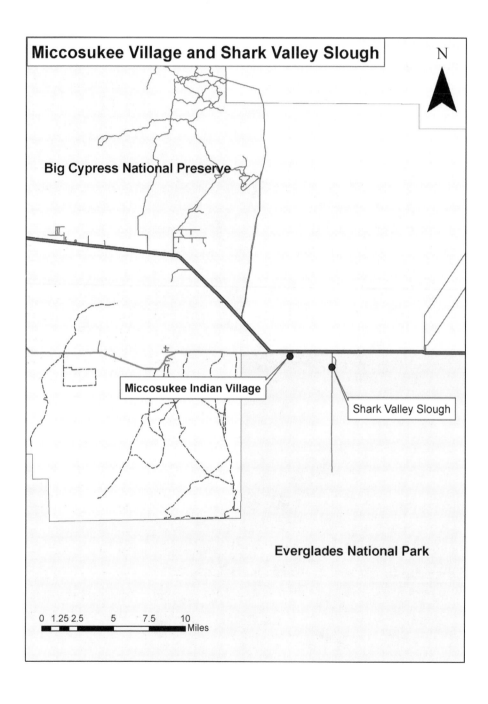

Getting There

While the size of the Everglades has been reduced by more than half since the days when the first Seminoles moved in, it is still an impressive wetland and there are several ways to experience it. For a tribal flavor, you can visit any number of Indian-operated airboat tours along U.S. 41, the Tamiami Trail, beginning about twenty miles west of Miami. Seminoles and Miccosukees began using airboats in the 1940s when they first became popular and they haven't looked back. An airboat ride enables you to zoom across the marshlands at high rates of speed and glimpse wading birds rising above the horizon and alligators diving into deeper waters.

The 1.5 million-acre Everglades National Park—the third largest in the lower 48 states—offers several ways to experience the River of Grass. You can take a guided tram ride along the Shark Valley Slough, or you can bike or walk. There is a 65-foot observation platform at the end of the slough that provides a panoramic view of the Everglades environment. The slough can be accessed from the Tamiami Trail along the park's northern boundary, just east of the Miccosukee Cultural Center.

The southern section of the park can best be accessed by driving to Homestead south of Miami and taking the scenic drive on Highway 9336 to Flamingo. There are several short hiking trails and overlooks, and canoes are available for rent in Flamingo. As a note of caution, the Everglades are best enjoyed in winter when bugs are more tolerable. To visit in summer is to marvel at how Seminoles and early pioneers tolerated insect swarms, and one better understands statements such as this by General Alexander Webb in 1855, "This country should be preserved for the Indians … and if the fleas and other vermin do not destroy them they might be left to live. I could not wish them all in a worse place."

To learn more about Everglades National Park, log onto http://www.nps.gov/ever/index.htm.

The 729,000-acre Big Cypress National Preserve along the northwest border of Everglades National Park is also worthy of exploration. The Florida National Scenic Trail begins (or ends) here, and it is a wet slog for most months of the year, although campsites are on dry tree islands. Don't like hiking in water? The preserve also features the Loop Road Scenic Drive off the Tamiami Trail along with several boardwalks and overlooks. Be sure to check in at the main visitor center along the Tamiami Trail for ranger-led activities. To learn more, log onto http://www.nps.gov/bicy/index.htm.

Fifteen

Touching Seminole Ways at Big Cypress

*The Seminole Trail moves into modern times with two popular Seminole attractions on the **Big Cypress Reservation** southwest of Lake Okeechobee—**Billie Swamp Safari** and the state-of-the-art **Ah-Tah-Thi-Ki Museum**. Both attractions juxtapose old and new so that visitors can become immersed in both Seminole culture and the area environment.*

Alligator wrestling, airboat rides, traditional arts and lifestyles … these were the attractions that lured visitors to Seminole Indian villages along Florida's Tamiami Trail and Alligator Alley through the twentieth century. Add to that the mystique of a people who survived prolonged wars and removal attempts by hiding in the vastness of North America's largest wetlands—the Everglades and Big Cypress Swamp. The roadside attractions were necessary because drainage had depleted the Everglades environment, diminishing wildlife populations, and thereby impacting the Seminoles' ability to live off the land and waters.

Along came high stakes-bingo in 1979. It was the beginning of a national Indian gaming trend, born in the swamps of Florida near metropolitan Miami. Within a few years, the Seminole Tribe of Florida was flush with money. Each member began receiving an allotment, and roadside tourist attractions were no longer necessary. The tribe took a step back and focused on what they wanted to offer visitors who were still curious about Seminole existence in the Sunshine State. Two main ideas began to gel. One was a world-class museum of Seminole history and culture, and the other would roll together several elements of early tourism venues into one main attraction.

After years of planning and effort, the tribal-sponsored Billie Swamp Safari and Ah-Tah-Thi-Ki Museum—only three miles apart— opened in the late 1990s on the Big Cypress Seminole Reservation in the heart of the Everglades/Big Cypress region. According to the tribe, the two venues reveal how the Seminole people have shifted their reliance on the Everglades "from one of natural resource utilization for survival to marketing the Everglades idea." The attractions are a form of "cultural tourism" that are "immersive," juxtaposing old and new.

The Billie Swamp Safari features wild animal shows, airboat and swamp buggy rides, and the reservation's only full-service restaurant. Every February, they put on the "Big Cypress Shootout." Reenactors portray Seminole warriors and United States soldiers engaged in a Second Seminole War skirmish in the 1830s. Typically in this Everglades environment, Seminole warriors skillfully used hit-and-run guerilla warfare tactics against superior numbers.

To explore the quieter side of Billie Swamp Safari, visitors can walk a boardwalk nature trail through part of a 2,100-acre tribal nature preserve. They can also stay in one of several screened cabins—minus electricity.

The rafters of the one-room cabins are made with shaved cypress poles in the traditional Seminole style of their open-air "chickees." Palm

Swamp buggy station at the Billie Swamp Safari on the Big Cypress Seminole Reservation south of Lake Okeechobee.

Chickee cabins for rent at the Billie Swamp Safari on the Big Cypress Seminole Reservation south of Lake Okeechobee.

fronds cover the roofs, each frond carefully folded over and layered in a pattern proven to repel rain. Raised wooden floors and soft beds replace the usual jungle hammocks or hard sleeping platforms. Screened sides keep out bugs, long curtains provide privacy, and oil lamps give off a warm glow. Most Seminoles now live in modern-style houses, but the chickee still holds a special place in their yards and in ceremonial and community centers. Now, visitors can taste the chickee experience.

Lying in bed, your eyes wander over the tight pattern of palm fronds above. You realize that Seminoles have gazed upon a similar scene for more than 175 years, from when the majority of Seminoles first emerged into the warm South Florida climate. The chickee was cooler and much easier to erect than a four-sided cabin, an important attribute for a people

Nighttime view of rafters inside a chickee cabin at the Billie Swamp Safari on the Big Cypress Seminole Reservation south of Lake Okeechobee.

on the move during the Second Seminole War. The chickee is similar to structures they used in more northern climates for storage shelters and for temporary hunting camps, and they may have refined the design with input from remnant Indians of other Florida tribes, or from Caribbean peoples. Elements of the chickee style are uniquely Seminole.

At the Billie Swamp Safari chickee cabins, the oil lamps allow for reading, writing, and reflection without the glaring distraction of television or computers. The palm fronds give off a sweet aroma, and the only sounds are those of insects, tree frogs, and the occasional call of a night bird or other animal.

Outside, the overhead stars are magnificent. Ft. Lauderdale is fifty miles in one direction, Naples fifty miles in the other. Few other places in south Florida offer a night sky unfettered by the glow of distant lights. Just make sure to bring a flashlight for moving around outside or when you blow out the lantern. A central bath house is open all night.

There are two main rows of cabins at Billie Swamp Safari. One faces an open water swamp and the other row backs up to a thick cypress swamp. Both have their attributes.

Late at night, a barred owl may call from deep within the swamp. Usually another owl or three answer and together they begin a raucous council.

In the wee hours before dawn, if the curtains are open, first light filters ever slowly into the chickee cabin. Alligators bellow, wading birds croak, and the swamp slowly begins to awaken. The low overhang of feathery palm fronds keeps out some light, but sleeping in late can be difficult. The park opens at 9:30 a.m. to the daytime public, and airboats and swamp buggies will soon take visitors on adventures into the wild.

Ah-Tah-Thi-Ki Museum entrance on the Big Cypress Seminole Reservation.

"A Place to Learn"

Life-size displays of traditional Seminole life in the 1890s greet visitors at the Ah-Tah-Thi-Ki Museum, a name meaning "a place to learn, a place to remember" in the Miccosukee language. There is a night-time Green Corn Dance under the stars, a family traveling by dugout canoe, a traditional stickball game between men and women, a woman tanning a deerskin, women cooking in a chickee, and young boys hunting. Rooms display artifacts and showcase rotating exhibits, and a five-screen theater gives an overview of Seminole history, from the Seminole wars to the present day.

As if to symbolize the tribe's emergence into the twenty-first century, a Microsoft surface touch table beneath an indoor chickee roof enables visitors to select oral history recordings made by tribal members. One can sit back on a bench and listen to Seminole creation myths by William Cypress and various stories of growing up Seminole by Louise Gopher, Michael Tiger, James Billie, and others.

Perhaps the culmination of a museum visit is the 1.1-mile boardwalk behind the main building. It traverses a lush cypress swamp that is interspersed by willow heads, pond apple sloughs, and towering southern red maple trees. This gives the Ah-Tah-Thi-Ki Museum a clear advantage over big city museums. While the quantity of visitors may not be as high as if the museum had been built near downtown Miami or Naples, the experiential quality of learning about a people who had a special kinship with nature is especially relevant in this natural setting.

Signs along the boardwalk describe more than sixty different plants and their traditional medicinal and utilitarian uses in Seminole culture. For example, resurrection fern, a common plant that grows on large hardwood trees, is collected and boiled by the Seminoles as a concoction to treat depression. If a child eats the heart of a cabbage palm, it is believed that he or she will grow big and tall. The Seminoles treat diarrhea with several lichen species, and wax myrtle leaves and branches are used as a natural insecticide against fleas. Many of the time-proven medicinal plants are still used by Seminoles today, often in conjunction with modern medicines, and it is customary for their preparation to be made by a trained healer or medicine person. Liquid medicines are often "doctored" by a shaman blowing into the mixture with a cane tube, thereby aerating the medicine and infusing it with sacred breath.

The boardwalk leads visitors to a stop at the curators' building where they can glimpse coming attractions in the works. Seminole artifacts from the Smithsonian in Washington, D.C., and the Heye Museum in New York City are now coming back to the Seminole people through the nationally accredited Ah-Tah-Thi-Ki Museum.

The next destination along the boardwalk is a re-created ceremonial grounds, a traditional religious and political meeting place where four chickees aligned with the cardinal directions are arranged around a cleared area. A vertical cypress post represents the ballpost for the stickball game, a lacrosse-style game in which men often play women in trying to throw a small leather ball at the post. The men must use a webbed stick in each hand while the women can freely use their hands, helping to even the odds. The game is often played at the primary traditional Seminole ceremony, the Green Corn Dance, held in undisclosed south Florida locations in late spring or early summer.

The Green Corn Dance is a multi-day purification ritual that involves fasting, the taking of herbal medicines, and hours of dancing around a sacred fire. During the "stomp dances," a dance leader or medicine man creates the initial rhythm with a hand rattle while leading a spiraling line of men and women. The men verbally answer each of his exhortations and verses, while the women join in by rhythmically shuffling shakers—often made of turtle shells—strapped to their ankles. Other types of dances, such as those honoring different animals, are also performed. The primary purpose of the ceremony is to give thanks to Creator—the Maker of Breath—for providing food. It is also a time to settle tribal disputes and to recognize young men emerging into manhood.

Clans normally camp together and sit at designated spots at the Green Corn Dance and certain clans have specific ceremonial duties. As explained in one of the museum exhibits, Panther and Wind clan members make the medicines for the people. The reason harkens back to Seminole creation stories when Creator was creating the world. Creator liked to sit beside Panther and stroke his soft fur. He endowed Panther with special powers and wanted Panther to be the first to walk the Earth. The animals were underground and there was a small opening to the surface, but Panther could not squeeze through. Wind helped Panther by swirling around and around and

Lacrosse-style stickball game exhibit in the Ah-Tah-Thi-Ki Museum
on the Big Cypress Seminole Reservation.

making the opening larger. Ever since, Wind and Panther have been brothers, and Panther taught Wind knowledge and healing medicine.

Other Seminole clans are Bear, Big Town/Toad, Bird, Snake, Deer and Otter, while some historical clans, such as Alligator, are now extinct. A person's clan identity is passed down through the mother's side of the family. In traditional Seminole society, each clan had a *mekko* or chief, so it was rare for one person to speak for the entire tribe. Plus, women had a major leadership role, something early Europeans often sought to overlook. Custom forbade people from marrying within their own clan since they could be related by blood, and at one time, people could not marry outside of the tribe, although this is no longer the case. One must be one quarter Seminole to be a member of the tribe.

Adjacent to the museum's ceremonial grounds is the Seminole camp or village site. Visitors can step off the trail and duck under the low overhangs of palm-thatched chickees and watch Seminole bead workers and basket makers at work. "We get a lot of European visitors, especially Germans," said bead worker Lorraine Posada of the Seminole Wind Clan. "They like our flag [the Seminole medicine colors of white, black, red and yellow] because their flag colors are almost the same as ours except they don't have white." The four colors in the Seminole flag are symbolic of the four directions—white for south, black for north, red for west, and yellow for east.

Besides people, animals often visit the camp, although none of the shy Florida panthers have been seen. Raccoons are frequent guests and a bear once paid a surprise visit. "We had to close the camp for a few days until he went on his way," Posada said, laughing. At one time, the Seminoles might have killed and eaten the bear, and used its skin for warmth or for trade, its claws for jewelry, and its fat for cooking and mosquito protection.

The Seminole camp and ceremonial grounds are only a half mile down a boardwalk through a thick cypress swamp, but the feeling of

Beadmaker Lorraine Posada at the traditional camp of the Ah-Tah-Thi-Ki Museum on the Big Cypress Seminole Reservation.

remoteness and authenticity makes them seem deep in the wilderness and during an earlier time. The ceremonial grounds is not usually occupied—that's understandable. No one carries on the Green Corn Dance here, or cooks traditional medicine, or throws a small leather ball at the tall cypress pole. But the adjacent camp is inhabited by Seminole people during museum hours. It highlights another difference between Ah-Tah-Thi-Ki and those museums that passively depict people and life ways long gone.

"We hope the museum provides a slice of Seminole life and whets the appetite for visitors to want to know more," said Pedro Zepeda, the museum's traditional arts and outreach coordinator. "We want people to know that we are still here and not just in the history books."

At the camp, George Billie, an elder from the Panther Clan, works as the village groundskeeper. He keeps a fire burning beneath the thatched roof of one chickee with a traditional four-log design aligned with the cardinal directions. The logs are slowly pushed into the fire as needed. And like so many things at the museum, the old Seminole world comes alive here, and it all seems to fit with the lush foliage of the swamp forest. Birds sing, tree frogs call from chickee rafters, and the smell of smoke lingers on clothes like the unconquered Seminole spirit.

Getting There

The easiest way to reach both the Ah-Tah-Thi-Ki Museum and Billie Swamp Safari is to take Alligator Alley (I-75) either from the west or east to exit 49, about halfway between Naples and Fort Lauderdale. Head north about 16 miles, following signs to the Big Cypress Reservation. Signs point the way to both attractions. Native Americans receive free admission to the museum and active military personnel and their families receive a significant discount at Billie Swamp Safari.

Billie Swamp Safari is open every day of the year except Christ-

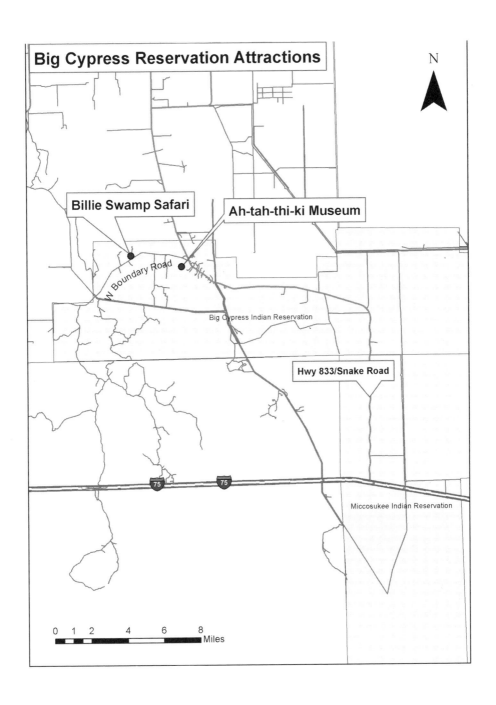

Big Cypress Reservation Attractions

N

Billie Swamp Safari

Ah-tah-thi-ki Museum

W Boundary Road

Big Cypress Indian Reservation

Hwy 833/Snake Road

75   75

Miccosukee Indian Reservation

0 1 2   4   6   8
Miles

mas from 9:30 a.m. to 6 p.m. To reserve the chickee cabins, call (800) 949-6101. The website is http://www.swampsafari.com/. The address is 30000 Gator Tail Trail, Clewiston, FL 33440; (863) 983-6101.

The Ah-Tah-Thi-Ki Museum is open from 9 a.m. to 5 p.m. every day of the year except for major holidays. Log onto http://www.ahtah thiki.com/ for more information. The address is 34725 W. Boundary Road, Clewiston, FL 33440; (877) 902-1113.

Sixteen
Casinos and Rock and Roll

Once chased relentlessly into the swamps of South Florida, with the vast majority of Seminoles being removed west of the Mississippi, the Seminole Tribe of Florida has emerged as one of the most prosperous tribes in North America. Indian gaming has transformed the Seminole landscape, and the Seminole Trail now takes us to several Florida venues that make up the primary Seminole economic engine.

An economic tsunami. There's no better way to summarize what happened to the Seminole Tribe of Florida since it inaugurated the first Native American high-stakes gambling facility in the United States in 1979—Hollywood Bingo. "I want to get away from defeatist thinking," tribal chairman James Billie said in his 1995 biography, *Chief.* "I want to build confidence among the tribe. Let the people get used to the idea that they are somebody, that they have culture, that they can achieve. I want to make sure they get the opportunity to do what they want... and not what somebody else wants."

Seminole Hard Rock Hotel and Casino entrance in Tampa.

The tribe now boasts six gaming attractions—"the new buffalo," as some call it—as well its own media company, travel agency, airport, building inspection office, veterans agency, library system, housing department, school, police, campground, and newspaper. The tribe also hosts several large annual festivals that are open to the public—the Seminole Tribal Fair in Hollywood on the second weekend in February, the American Indian Arts Celebration on the Big Cypress Reservation in early November, and the Big Cypress Shootout Second Seminole War Reenactment at Billie Swamp Safari in February. There are also various rodeo events at the Fred Smith Arena on the Brighton Reservation.

In December 2006, the tribe purchased Hard Rock International, a chain of high-profile restaurants and casinos, for $965 million. The deal covered about two-thirds of the Hard Rock empire and it is thought to be the largest business transaction by a Native American tribe. "We're going to buy Manhattan back, one hamburger at a time," joked tribal representative Max Osceola Jr. when the deal was announced. With the purchase, the Seminoles likely own the largest collection of rock and roll memorabilia in the world!

The Miccosukee Tribe of Florida, with about 650 enrolled members and four main reservation areas, has one casino near Miami that boasts 1,900 gaming machines. The tribe also has a golf course, police department, museum, Indian village, clinic, day care center, resort and convention center, and a tobacco shop.

To enter one of the tribal casinos is a case of sensory overload. Rows of digital slot machines light up vast rooms, most manned by people with digital expense cards. Gone are the days of the hand-cranked "one-armed bandits." There are also no bells and whistles and the rush of coins to a slot for winners. One can win—or lose—quietly. There are also blackjack tables, poker rooms, and stages for performers. And in the case of the Seminole Hard Rock casinos, rock and roll music is constantly playing.

Near the Seminole casino entrances, traditional Seminole statues and displays are juxtaposed beside framed curios from rock and roll musicians. At the Hard Rock gift shop in Tampa, a Seminole storekeeper was asked if a particular Seminole elder in the area ever visited the casino. "Oh, once in a while he comes in for a meeting," she said with a wry smile. Having grown up in a traditional village, he likely felt that the casino was just a bit too far from his comfort zone.

Times have certainly changed for Florida's Seminoles and Miccosukees, especially economically. What does it mean for their culture and future? Since gaming is a fairly new phenomenon, it may be too early to tell. Some point to a lack of motivation among young people due to high monthly dividends—and subsequent materialism, alcoholism and accidents. Others wonder about the ethics of promoting gambling. "The money does help out the people, but what is the process?" asks Samuel Tommie in *Seminole Voices*. "The process is, if we are doing gambling, then there are people being addicted to gambling and it might be bad for their families. So economy is a very funny thing. I wish things were different. I guess it is a big rat race or else we would not be in gambling."

Anthropologist Anthony J. Paredes observed in 1995: "There is, indeed, a certain irony if not paradox in the fact that it was the Seminoles, so long respected for clinging to the 'ways of their ancestors' in the swampy vastness of the Everglades, who would be so pivotal in unleashing the juggernaut of Indian gaming in modern America."

Some point out that monthly dividend checks from Indian gaming proceeds (up to $120,000 annually per member in 2007) has sapped the motivation of tribal members to work, promoting a more sedentary and unhealthy lifestyle. Many Seminoles face challenges with drug and alcohol abuse, diabetes, obesity and other health problems. Of course, these problems are also faced by many in the dominant culture. On the other hand, gaming proceeds have opened up educational opportunities for Seminole youth and adults that were never available before, along

Entrance to the Miccosukee Casino near Miami.

with new health and social services. The Seminole Tribe of Florida's Ahfachkee School, for example, on the Big Cypress Reservation, is a state-of-the-art educational facility that features multi-lingual education and numerous special programs, events, and field trips. It is one of the few accredited tribal-run schools on the continent.

Gaming revenues have also allowed the tribe to develop cultural attractions for tourists such as the Ah-Tah-Thi-Ki Museum and the Billie Swamp Safari (see previous chapter). Jeanette Cypress, speaking in *Seminole Voices,* spoke favorably of the attractions. "I think it is a good public image, too. I do not want everybody to think, all they do is casinos and gambling and bingo. They do not realize that we have citrus and cattle and we are normal like everybody else. I have had people think that we do not pay taxes, that everything is for free, and they are in shock to know that we have to pay for everything. . . . We might have the cultural things that are a little different, but still, basically, we all have the same problems."

Florida State University History Professor Dr. Andrew Frank has a unique perspective on the Seminole Indian gaming phenomenon. "Rather than destroy culture as we are prone to believe, gaming and other of what we would call capitalist ventures, reinforce or allow it," he said in a 2011 lecture. "In many ways, as the phrase 'renaissance' would have us believe, Seminole culture today is stronger than it was thirty or forty years ago. This is not as one-sided as I would present and there are certainly struggles that modern native peoples are going to face and continue to face, but if we put it on balance, the problems caused by having money are significantly less important than the solutions that money creates. And if we can think about the implications in our own heads of what it means that we long for the day when Seminoles were poor because they could have their culture, I think we get to the point where we are uneasy. And we can replace Seminole with virtually any other Native American tribe that has seen recent success. . . . I'd like to remind you that Seminoles today are still Seminoles and many of the things that enable them to imagine themselves being Seminoles tomorrow, and in twenty or fifty or one hundred years, come from that optimism that the modern and traditional can be the same."

Frank posed the question about what constitutes a tradition, pointing out that the main things we think about regarding traditional Seminole culture all happened within the last two hundred years—the chickee, alligator wrestling, and patchwork clothing. While the chickee is still in use more often for social, family, and cultural gatherings, few Seminoles or Miccosukees still engage in alligator wrestling, and patchwork clothing continues to evolve. At a recent Seminole fair, there were three categories for the clothing contest—traditional wear, modern wear, and modern traditional wear. Other forms of Seminole art vary widely, from the paintings of Noah Billie that portray early Seminole life to the country twang of James Billie and his band. Basketry has also evolved, with more elaborate styles introduced by the Deaconess Harriet Bedell in the 1930s and by Mrs. Edith Boehmer in the two decades that followed. The styles and colors used by Seminole basket makers continue to intrigue and attract collectors.

Historian Jon Grandage in a 2012 lecture pointed out one constant of Seminole culture that has remained even after five hundred years of contact with European and African cultures: "The Seminoles were largely matrilineal until the second half of the twentieth century, despite pressures from the outside to change, and some still follow the traditional pattern of social organization." Seminole clans move through the mother's side to the children and Seminole men often move into the camps or household areas of the wife's family. The pattern was altered for some families by government housing programs and by cattle programs that were initially for men only.

Other aspects of Seminole life have obviously evolved, and Grandage added, "We think of Native American cultures as having reached a point

Sign for Seminole cattle operation on the Big Cypress Seminole Reservation.

of completion—they only existed in the past—but the Seminoles went through a process of change and adaptation. There is not an end to this process."

The Seminole Trail, then, does not have an end. It continues to be blazed by a culture and tribe boldly facing the twenty-first century, and if this book were revised in fifty or a hundred years hence, there would certainly be new stops along the way. And all of them would be distinctly Seminole.

Getting There

The Seminole Tribe of Florida currently has six gaming facilities. The largest is the Seminole Hard Rock Hotel and Casino in Hollywood. The attraction boasts 500 hotel rooms, 130,000 square feet of casino space, two parking garages, a 6,000-seat arena, the Okalee Indian Village, and an outdoor mall called "Seminole Paradise." It is located just off State Road 7 (U.S. Highway 441) north of Stirling Road in Hollywood and is visible from the Florida Turnpike. The address is 5716 Seminole Way, Hollywood, 33314; (800) 683-7800.

Inside the Hollywood Seminole Hard Rock Hotel and Casino.

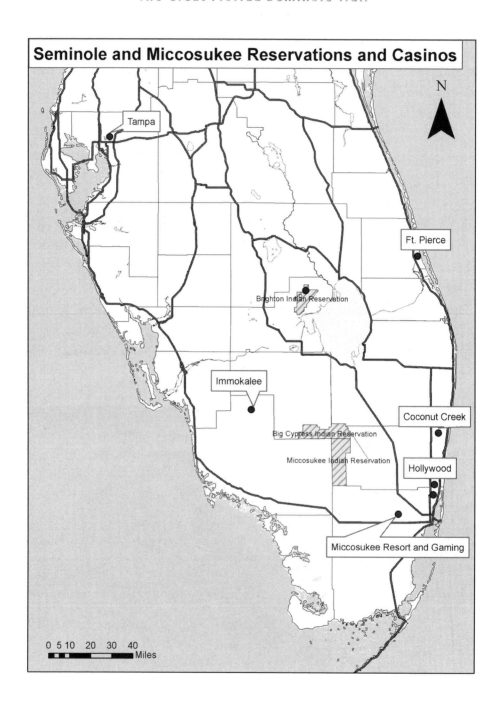

Seminole and Miccosukee Reservations and Casinos

N

Tampa

Ft. Pierce

Brighton Indian Reservation

Immokalee

Coconut Creek

Big Cypress Indian Reservation

Miccosukee Indian Reservation

Hollywood

Miccosukee Resort and Gaming

0 5 10 20 30 40
Miles

The Seminole Casino Hollywood, opened in 1979, was the first high-stakes Native American–owned operation in the country. After numerous court challenges, the gaming era on Indian reservations began. The attraction currently features round-the-clock poker on 48 tables and "Lightning Bingo"—accelerated games that are like the old church games on steroids. The address is 4150 North State Road 7, Hollywood, 33024; (866) 2-Casino.

Seminole Casino Coconut Creek features more than 1,500 Vegas-style and bingo-style slot machines along with restaurants and a lounge.

Seminole Casino Brighton on the Brighton Reservation northwest of Lake Okeechobee features High Stakes Bingo, slot machines, poker, and electronic blackjack. Located between State Road 78 and State Road 70 on Highway 721, the address is 17735 Reservation Road, Okeechobee, 34974; (863) 467-9998.

Southwest Florida's Seminole Casino Immokalee features poker, gaming machines, and a restaurant and bar. The address is 506 South First Street, Immokalee, 34142; (800) 218-0007.

The Seminole Hard Rock Hotel and Casino in Tampa features a 190,000-square-foot gaming floor containing several hundred slot machines, various table games, and a poker room. It is located just off Interstate 4 at North Orient Road. The address is 5223 N. Orient Road, Tampa, 33610; (866) 502-7529.

The Miccosukee Resort and Gaming between Miami and the Everglades features 1,900 gaming machines, a 1,050-seat high-stakes bingo hall, a 32-table poker room, restaurants, and a hotel. Frequent sporting events and parties along with the annual Miccosukee Everglades Music Festival and other events are held at the adjacent 1,200-seat Miccosukee Entertainment Dome. The address is 500 S.W. 177th Avenue, Miami, 33194; (877) 242-6464.

All of the casinos are open 24 hours a day, seven days a week.

Bibliography

Anderson, Lars. *Paynes Prairie: A History of the Great Savanna.* Sarasota: Pineapple Press, 2001.

Annino, Jan Godown. *She Sang Promise: The Story of Betty Mae Jumper, Seminole Tribal Leader.* Washington, D.C.: National Geographic, 2010.

Barbour, Thomas. *That Vanishing Eden.* Boston: Little, Brown and Company, 1944.

Bemrose, John. *Reminiscences of the Second Seminole War.* Gainesville: University Press of Florida, 1966.

Blank, Joan Gill. *Key Biscayne: A History of Miami's Tropical Island and the Cape Florida Lighthouse.* Sarasota: Pineapple Press, 1996.

Buchanan, Robert C. "A Journal of Lt. Robert C. Buchanan During the Seminole War," *Florida Historical Quarterly,* October 1950 #2, Volume XXIX, pages 132–151.

Cox, Dale. *The Early History of Gadsden County.* Self-published, Bascom, FL: 2008.

de Quesada, Alejandro M. Jr. *The Men of Fort Foster.* Union City, TN: Pioneer Press, 1996.

Dodd, Dorothy. "Jacob Housman of Indian Key," *Tequesta Number VIII* (1948), 3–19.

Downs, Dorothy. *Art of the Florida Seminole and Miccosukee Indians.* Gainesville: University Press of Florida, 1995.

Downs, Dorothy. *Patchwork: Seminole and Miccosukee Art and Activities.* Sarasota: Pineapple Press, 2005.

Eaton, Sarah E. "Fort Dallas Designation Report," City of Miami, 11/4/1983.

Ennemoser, Rusty. "Florida's History in Stone: The Great Sugar Mill Plantations," *Florida Heritage,* Spring 1997, pages 18–21.

Fehrman, Jan. "Stepping Back in Time with Dowling Watford," *Okeechobee,* Winter 2010, pages 26–30.

Francke, Arthur E. Jr. *Coacoochee: Made of the Sands of Florida.* DeLeon Springs: E.O. Painter Printing, 1986.

Giddings, Joshua R. *The Exiles of Florida.* Columbus: Follett, Foster and Co., 1858.

Glenn, James Lafayette. *My Work among the Florida Seminoles.* Orlando: University Presses of Florida, 1982.

Grunwald, Michael. *The Swamp: The Everglades, Florida, and the Politics of Paradise.* New York: Simon & Schuster, 2006.

Hann, John H. *Apalachee, The Land Between the Rivers.* Gainesville: University Presses of Florida, 1988.

____, and Bonnie G. McEwan. *The Apalachee Indians and Mission San Luis.* Gainesville: University Press of Florida, 1998.

Heidler, David S., and Jeanne T. Heidler. *Old Hickory's War: Andrew Jackson and the Quest for Empire*. Mechanicsburg, PA: Stackpole Books, 1996.

Henshall, James A. *Camping and Cruising in Florida*. Cincinnati: Robert Clarke, 1884.

Hiaasen, Carl. *Tourist Season*. New York: Warner Books, 1987.

Jumper, Betty Mae Tiger, and Patsy West. *A Seminole Legend: The Life of Betty Mae Tiger Jumper*. Gainesville: University Press of Florida, 2001.

Kersey, Harry A. *The Stranahans of Fort Lauderdale*. Gainesville: University Press of Florida, 2003.

___, and Julian M. Pleasants. *Seminole Voices: Reflections on Their Changing Society, 1970–2000*. Lincoln and London: University of Nebraska Press, 2010.

Krantz, Matt. "Seminole Tribe of Florida Buys Hard Rock Cafes, Hotels, Casinos," *USA Today* website article 12/7/2006, accessed 11/23/11, http://www.usatoday.com/money/industries/food/2006-12-07-seminoles-hardrock_x.htm.

Laumer, Frank, ed. *Amidst a Storm of Bullets: The Diary of Lt. Henry Prince in Florida 1836–1842*. Tampa: University of Tampa Press, 1998.

Laumer, Frank. *Dade's Last Command*. Gainesville: University Press of Florida, 1995.

____. *Nobody's Hero*. Sarasota: Pineapple Press, 2008.

Mahon, John. *History of the Second Seminole War 1835–1842, Revised Edition*. Gainesville: University Press of Florida, 1985.

Missal, John, and Mary Lou Missall. *The Seminole Wars*. Gainesville: University Press of Florida, 2004.

Monk, J. Floyd. "Christmas Day in Florida, 1837," *Tequesta Number XXXVIII* (1978), 5–38.

Moore-Willson, Minnie. *The Seminoles of Florida.* New York: Moffat, Yard and Company, 1896, 1910, 1911, Third Reading.

Motte, J.R. *Journey into Wilderness.* Gainesville: University of Florida Press, 1963.

Oeffner, Barbara. *Chief, Champion of the Everglades: A Biography of Seminole Chief James Billie.* Palm Beach: Cape Cod Writers, Inc., 1995.

O'Neal, Maston. *Prologue.* Self-published, 1985.

Paisley, Clifton. *The Red Hills of Florida, 1528–1865.* Tuscaloosa: University of Alabama Press, 1989.

Pickard, John B. *Florida's Eden: An Illustrated History of Alachua County.* Gainesville: Maupin House, 1994.

Proby, Kathryn Hall. *Audubon in Florida.* Coral Gables: University of Miami Press, 1974.

Robinson, Ralph T. "Henry Perrine, Pioneer Horticulturist of Florida," *Tequesta Number 11* (1942), 16–24.

Schene, Michael G. "History of Fort Foster," Florida Division of Parks and Recreation, July 1974.

_____. "Indian Key," *Tequesta Number XXXVI* (1976), 3–27.

Snow, Alice Micco, and Susan Enns Stans. *Healing Plants: Medicine of the Florida Seminole Indians.* Gainesville: University Press of Florida, 2001.

Spornick, Charles D., Alan R. Cattier, and Robert J. Greene. *An Outdoor Guide to Bartram's Travels.* Athens: University of Georgia Press, 2003.

Sturtevant, William C. "A Seminole Personal Document," *Tequesta Number XVI* (1956), 55–75.

____. "Chakaika and the 'Spanish Indians,'" *Tequesta Number XIII* (1953), 35–73.

Tebeau, Charlton W. *The Story of the Chokoloskee Bay Country.* Miami: University of Miami Press, 1955.

Tiger, Buffalo, and Harry A. Kersey, Jr. *Buffalo Tiger: A Life in the Everglades.* Lincoln and London: University of Nebraska Press, 2002.

Van Doran, Mark, ed. *Travels of William Bartram.* New York: Dover Publications, 1928, 1955.

Walker, Hester Perrine. "The Perrines at Indian Key, Florida, 1838–1840," *Tequesta Number VII* (1947), 69–78.

Waselkov, Gregory A., and Kathryn E. Holland Braund. *William Bartram on the Southeastern Indians.* Lincoln and London: University of Nebraska Press, 1995.

Weisman, Brent Richards. *Like Beads on a String.* Tuscaloosa: University of Alabama Press, 1989.

____. *Unconquered People: Florida's Seminole and Miccosukee Indians.* Gainesville: University Press of Florida, 1999.

West, Patsy. *The Enduring Seminoles: From Alligator Wrestling to Casino Gaming, Revised and Expanded Edition.* Gainesville: University Press of Florida, 1998, 2008.

Wickman, Patricia Riles. *The Tree that Bends: Discourse, Power, and the Survival of Maskoki People.* Tuscaloosa: University of Alabama Press, 1999.

Willoughby, Hugh L. *Across the Everglades: A Canoe Journey of Exploration.* Port Salerno, FL: Florida Classics Library, 1898, 1992.

Interviews

Bennett, Gilmer. Written correspondence, 2006

Burney, Harvard. Okeechobee Battlefield, 2011

Burney, Laney. Okeechobee Battlefield, 2011

Cabrera, Carlos. Miccosukee Indian Village, 2012

Frank, Dr. Andrew. Tallahassee Writer's Conference lecture, 2011

Grandage, Jon. Lecture at Mission San Luis, 2012

Griffin, John. Dade Battlefield, 2011

Griffin, Matthew. Dade Battlefield, 2011

Johns, Mary. Tallahassee, 2000

Jumper, Moses Jr. Dade Battlefield, 2011

Posada, Lorraine. Ah-Tah-Thi-Ki Museum, Big Cypress Reservation, 2011

Zepeda, Pedro. Okeechobee Battlefield, 2011

Index

Numbers in *italics* represent illustrations. m = map

216

Index

219

Francis Town, 39
Frank, Dr. Andrew, 204–205
Fred Smith Arena, 201
Freeman, Ethel Cutler, 167
Friends of the Florida Seminoles, 151
Friends of the Seminoles, 151
Friar Paiva, 4–6
Frostproof (FL), 70, 72
Frostproof Historical Museum, 70, 72

Gadsden County (FL), 29
Gadsden, James, 29, 39
Gaines, Major General Edmund P., 27, 33, 37
Gainesville, 23–24, 127
Garcon, 28
Gardiner, Captain George W., 48–50, 56
Gatlin, Dr. John Slade, 50, 56
Geneva (FL), 131
Geneva Historical and Genealogical Society, 131
Gentry, Colonel Richard, 97–99
Georgia, 33
Georgia Militia, 38–39
Giddings, Joshua, 33
Gilliam, Captain Cornelius, 99
Glass, James, 113
Glenn, James Lafayette, 152
Gooden, Chebon, *54*
Gopher, Louise, 191
Grandage, Jon, 205–206
Green Corn Ceremony, 87, 162
Griffin, John, 57
Griffin, Matthew, 58, *58*
Groveland (FL), 57

Gulf of Mexico, 17

Halifax River, 81
Hann, John, 5–6
Hard Rock International, 201
Harney, Colonel William S., 113, 119, 136, 140
Harris, Buckner, 20
Healing Plants: Medicine of the Florida Seminole Indians (Snow and Stans), 14
Henshall, James A., 149
Hiaasen, Carl, 143
Hillsborough River, 62, 64
Hillsborough River State Park, 62, 65, *71m*, 72
Himollemico, 39
Historic Dunlawton Sugar Mill Gardens, 83
Hitchiti, 8, 13
Hollywood Seminole Reservation, 168
Horse, John, 85–86, 97
Housman, Jacob, 109–110, 113, 119
Huff, Sam, 166

Independent Traditional Seminole Nation, 168
Indian Key, 109–121, *110, 112, 118*
Indian Key Historic State Park, 119, *120m*, 121
Indian Key Raid, 109–121
Indian Law Resource Center, 168
Indian Removal Act, 46
Indian Territory. *See* Oklahoma
Inverness (FL), 59, 129
Jackson, Andrew: Battle of New Orleans, 20; First Seminole

Micanopy Historical Society
Museum and Archives, 21
Miccosukee, historic village of,
38–39
Miccosukee Indians, 13, 149, 167
Miccosukee language, 166
Miccosukee Indian Reservation,
208m
Miccosukee Indian Village, 161, *168,*
169–174, *171, 174, 182m*
Miccosukee Resort and Gaming,
203, 208m, 209
Miccosukee Tribe of Florida, 167,
201
Miramar (FL), 140
Missouri Legislature, 103
Missouri Volunteers, 96–98, 102
Mission San Luis, 1–11, *3, 9, 10m*
Mississippi River, 46
Mobile, AL, 7
Monk, J. Floyd, 98
Montgomery (AL), vii
Montgomery Advertiser, vii
Moore, James, 6, 39
Moore-Willson, Minnie, 84, 92,
165–166, 149–151
Moral, Fray Alonso, 6
Motte, Jacob Rhett, 62, 74–76, 78,
85–87, 102
Moultrie Creek, Treaty of, vii
Musa Isle Indian Village, 162, *162*
Muscogee Creek Indians. *See* Creek
Indians
Muscogee language, 166
Museum of Florida History, 123,
124m
*My Work among the Florida
Seminoles* (Glenn), 152

Nash, Roy, 163
National Trust for Historic
Preservation, 104
Neamathla, vii
National Register of Historic Places,
21
National Underground Railroad
Network to Freedom Site, 143
Negro Fort, 25–34, 39. *See also* Fort
Gadsden
Newnan, Colonel Daniel, 19
Newnan's Lake, 19, 21
New Orleans, 27, 97
New Smyrna Beach (FL), 83
New Smyrna Sugar Mill, 83
New York, 111

Ocala, vii
Ochlockonee River, 39
Okalee Indian Village, 161, 168–169,
173m, 174
Okeechobee Magazine, 105
Okeechobee, 95, 105, 108
Okeechobee Battlefield Friends,
104–105
Okeechobee Battlefield Historic
State Park, 95–96, *107m*
Okefenokee, 59
Oklahoma, vii, 59, 86, 136, 138, 149,
175
Oklahoma Seminoles, 175
Old Town. *See* Suwannee Old Town
Orlando, 65, 133
Osceola, 20, 47, 84–86
Osceola's Gardens, 162
Osceola's Indian Village, 162
Osceola, Max, Jr., 201
Octiarche, 125

Loxahatchee River battles, 136, 138; origins of, 46; San Felasco Hammock battle, 127; and Snake Warrior's Island, 138, 140; and Spanish Indians, 111, 113; sugar plantation destruction along East Coast, 73–83; and Tallahassee, v

Seminole Casino Brighton, *208m*, 209

Seminole Casino Coconut Creek, *208m*, 209

Seminole Casino Immokalee, *208m*, 209

Seminole Casino Hollywood, *208m*, 209

Seminole Hard Rock Hotel and Casino Tampa, *200*, 202, *208m*, 209

Seminole Hard Rock Hotel and Casino Hollywood, *173m, 207, 208m*, 209

Seminole Indians. *See also* Black Seminoles and Oklahoma Seminoles: and alligator wrestling, 162–165, 169–170; ball game of, 4; Brighton Seminoles, 150; and Everglades destruction, 165–166, 180–181; and gaming, 169, 172, 186, 199–209; gigging fish, 155; Green Corn Ceremony of, 162; early villages of 14–18; foods of, 47, 105–106, 148; medicines of, 4, 16–17, 191; mention of, 30; and Negro Fort, 26; origins of, 2, 7–9, 12–14; origins of name, 2, 14; and Pine

Island area, 150–151; post war lifestyle, 148–149; removal of, viii, 46, 59, 136, 138; spiritual beliefs of, 30–31, 87–88; statues of, 123, *123*; and Tamiami Trail completion, 156, 166–167; and tourist trade, 161–165, 168–172; trade practices of, 148–156

Seminole Legend, A (Jumper and West), 136, 138, 151–152, 164–165

Seminole Tribe of Florida, 13–14, 21, 105, 140, 165, 167, 199

Seminole Voices (Kersey, Jr., and Pleasants), 170, 202, 204

Seminoles of Florida, The (Moore-Willson), 84, 92, 165–166, 149–151

Seventh Calvary, 53

Shark Valley Slough, 151, *176, 180, 182m*, 183

Sixth Infantry (Battle of Okeechobee), 99–100

Smallwood Store, 148, 152–154, *154*, 156, *157m*, 158, *158*

Smallwood, Thelma, 153–154

Snake Warrior's Island Natural Area, 138 *139m*, 140

Snow, Alice, *Healing Plants: Medicine of the Florida Seminole Indians*, 14

South Carolina, 91

South Florida Sun Sentinel, 169

Spain: First Seminole War period, 26, 30, 32, 37; hatred of by Seminoles, 14; horses of, 53; missionaries of, 1–9

Spanish Indians, 111, 113

If you enjoyed reading this book, here are some other books from Pineapple Press on related topics. To request a catalog or to place an order, visit our website at www. pineapplepress.com. Or write to Pineapple Press, P.O. Box 3889, Sarasota, Florida 34230, or call 1-800-PINEAPL (746-3275).

FLORIDA HISTORY

Native Americans in Florida by Kevin M. McCarthy. A clear and concise telling of the history of the native peoples of Florida. Includes a calendar of important dates and the 185 sites on the Native American Heritage Trail.

St. Augustine and St. Johns County: A Historical Guide by William R. Adams. More than 80 of the oldest historic sites in and around the Ancient City of St. Augustine, from Fort San Diego in the north to the Dixie Highway in the south. Maps, directions, visitor information, and accurate historical narrative by a well-known St. Augustine historian.

Discovering the Civil War in Florida: A Reader and Guide, Second Edition by Paul Taylor. This important book for those interested in the Civil War in Florida has been updated and enhanced in this new edition. Its popularity rests on the inclusion of official government reports as well as firsthand reports by soldiers on both sides. Maps show locations of major battles and skirmishes. Both land and sea maneuvers are chronicled. The guide for visiting Florida's Civil War sites has been updated, and several sites have been added.

Presidents in Florida by James C. Clark. U.S. Presidents have played a major role in shaping Florida, whether waging wars, protecting the environment, seeking votes, or just drawing media attention to the state's attractions. Andrew Jackson came to fight Indians when *La Florida* was still a Spanish colony and then became the first territorial governor. Abraham Lincoln came up with the plan to get Florida back into the Union in 1864 to help his reelection chances. Ulysses S. Grant came to promote steamships on the St. Johns River. Regular visitors have included Calvin Coolidge, Herbert Hoover, Franklin Roosevelt, Richard Nixon, and John F. Kennedy.

Paynes Prairie: The Great Savanna, Second Edition by Lars Andersen. This new paperback edition of Paynes Prairie still offers the sweeping history of the shallow-bowl basin in the middle of Florida, just south of Gainesville, but now adds a guide to outdoor activities that can be enjoyed in the state preserve today, along with maps of trails for biking, hiking, and canoeing.

Historical Traveler's Guide to Florida, Second Edition by Eliot Kleinberg. From Fort Pickens in the Panhandle to Fort Jefferson in the ocean 40 miles beyond Key West, historical travelers will find many adventures waiting for them in Florida. Eliot Kleinberg—whose vocation, avocation, and obsession is Florida history—has poked around the state looking for the most fascinating historic places to visit. In this new updated edition, he presents 74 of his favorites—17 of them are new to this edition, and the rest have been completely updated.

Time Traveler's Guide to Florida by Jack Powell. A unique guidebook that describes 70 places and reenactments in Florida where you can experience the past, and a few where you can time-travel into the future.

Florida's Past: People and Events that Shaped the State by Gene Burnett. The three volumes in this series are chock-full of carefully researched, eclectic essays written in Gene Burnett's easygoing style. Many of these essays on Florida history were originally published in *Florida Trend* magazine.

200 Quick Looks at Florida History by James C. Clark. Florida has a complex and very interesting history, but few of us have time to read it in depth. So here are 200 quick looks at Florida's 10,000 years of history, from the arrival of the first natives to the present. The distilled version is packed with unusual and little-known facts and stories. An indispensable guide for Florida students, newcomers, and old-timers alike.

HISTORICAL FICTION

The Bucket Flower by Donald Robert Wilson. In 1893, 23-year-old Elizabeth Sprague goes into the Everglades to study its unique plant life, even though she's warned that a pampered "bucket flower" like her can't endure the rigors of the swamp. She encounters wild animals and even wilder men but finds her own strength and a new future.

Black Creek: The Taking of Florida by Paul Varnes. Through the story of one family, we learn how white settlers moved into the Florida territory, taking it from the natives— who had been there only a few generations—with false treaties and finally all-out war. Thus, both sides were newcomers anxious to "take Florida."

Confederate Money by Paul Varnes. In 1861, as this novel opens, a Confederate dollar is worth 90 cents. We follow Henry Fern as he fights on both sides of the war. Through shrewd dealings, he manages to amass $40,000 in Confederate paper money and finally changes his paper fortune into silver and gold.

For God, Gold and Glory by E. H. Haines. The riveting account of the invasion of the American Southeast from 1539 to 1543 by Hernando de Soto, as told by his private secretary, Rodrigo Ranjel. A meticulously researched tale of adventure and survival and the dark aspects of greed and power.

Nobody's Hero by Frank Laumer. Based on the true adventure of an American soldier who refused to die in spite of terrible wounds sustained during the battle known as Dade's Massacre, which started the Second Seminole War in Florida.

NOVELS BY PATRICK SMITH

A Land Remembered. In this best-selling novel of Florida, three generations of the MacIvey clan battle the hardships of the frontier to rise from a dirt-poor Cracker life to the wealth and standing of real estate tycoons.

Forever Island. A classic novel of the Everglades, *Forever Island* tells the story of Charlie Jumper, a Seminole Indian who clings to the old ways and teaches them to his grandson.

Allapattah. Toby Tiger is a young Seminole living in despair in the white man's world. He must wrestle the allapattah, or crocodile, to free himself.

The River Is Home. Smith's first novel revolves around a Mississippi family's struggle to cope with changes in their rural environment. Poor in material possessions, Skeeter's kinfolk are rich in their appreciation of their beautiful natural surroundings.

Angel City is the powerful and moving exposé of migrant workers in Florida in the 1970s. It was made into a critically acclaimed TV movie.

CRACKER WESTERNS

Alligator Gold by Janet Schrader. On his way home at the end of the Civil War, Caleb Hawkins is focused on getting back to his Florida cattle ranch. But along the way, Hawk encounters a very pregnant Madelaine Wilkes and learns that his only son has gone missing and that his old nemesis, Snake Barber, has taken over his ranch.

Bridger's Run by Jon Wilson. Tom Bridger has come to Florida in 1885 to find his long-lost uncle and a hidden treasure. It all comes down to a boxing match between Tom and the Key West Slasher.

Riders of the Suwannee by Lee Gramling. Tate Barkley returns to 1870s Florida just in time to come to the aid of a young widow and her children as they fight to save their homestead from outlaws.

Ghosts of the Green Swamp by Lee Gramling. Saddle up your easy chair and kick back for a Cracker Western featuring that rough-and-ready but soft-hearted Florida cowboy, Tate Barkley, introduced in *Riders of the Suwannee.*

Guns of the Palmetto Plains by Rick Tonyan. As the Civil War explodes over Florida, Tree Hooker dodges Union soldiers and Florida outlaws to drive cattle to feed the starving Confederacy.

Thunder on the St. Johns by Lee Gramling. Riverboat gambler Chance Ramsay teams up with the family of young Josh Carpenter and the trapper's daughter Abby Macklin to combat a slew of greedy outlaws seeking to destroy the dreams of honest homesteaders.

Trail from St. Augustine by Lee Gramling. A young trapper, a crusty ex-sailor, and an indentured servant girl fleeing a cruel master join forces to cross the Florida wilderness in search of buried treasure and a new life.

Wiregrass Country by Herb and Muncy Chapman. Set in 1835, this historical novel will transport you to a time when Florida settlers were few and laws were scarce. Meet the Dovers, a family of homesteaders determined to survive against all odds and triumph against the daily struggles that accompany running a cattle ranch.

THE HONOR SERIES

"Sign on early and set sail with Peter Wake for both solid historical context and exciting sea stories." —U.S. Naval Institute Proceedings

The Honor Series of naval fiction by Robert N. Macomber covers the life and career of American naval officer Peter Wake from 1863 to 1907. The first book in the series, *At the Edge of Honor,* won Best Historical Novel from the Florida Historical Society. The second, *Point of Honor,* won the Cook Literary Award for Best Work in Southern Fiction. The sixth, *A Different Kind of Honor,* won the Boyd Literary Award for Excellence in Military Fiction from the American Library Association.